ORIGAMI FOR THE ENTHUSIAST

STEP-BY-STEP INSTRUCTIONS IN OVER 700 DIAGRAMS

25 Original Projects by
JOHN MONTROLL

Dover Publications, Inc.
New York

Dedicated to
LILLIAN OPPENHEIMER
and
ALICE GRAY

FOREWORD

One of the charms of origami is that it appeals equally to the rawest beginner and the most skillful expert. Since beginners vastly out-number experts, almost all origami books are designed for them. Here at last is a book for experts only. It contains nothing that is not new and of a challenging difficulty.

The author, John Montroll, is a phenomenon among paperfolders. Scorning adult assistance, he mastered his first origami book at the age of six. At fourteen, when he first became an associate of the Origami Center of America, he was already a creative folder of great promise. Now, at twenty-seven, he is a University of Michigan graduate student of mathematics and one of this country's few truly original and distinguished authors of origami.

His personal preference is for complex models. Animals are diffi-cult subjects for the paperfolder—they have so many appendages—and Montroll's animals are more detailed than is usual in origami. Making one is a test of skill and concentration: but when well done, the result is so beautiful that it is worth the time and effort expended in the accomplishment. Happy folding.

LILLIAN OPPENHEIMER
Founder and Director,
The Origami Center of America

ALICE GRAY
Editor, *The Origamian*

Published in Canada by General Publishing Company, Ltd., 30 Lesmill Road, Don Mills, Toronto, Ontario.
Published in the United Kingdom by Constable and Com-pany, Ltd., 10 Orange Street, London WC2H 7EG.

Origami for the Enthusiast is a new work, first published by Dover Publications, Inc., in 1979.

International Standard Book Number: 0-486-23799-0
Library of Congress Catalog Card Number: 79-50425

Manufactured in the United States of America
Dover Publications, Inc.
180 Varick Street
New York, N.Y. 10014

INTRODUCTION

Origami is a challenging and unusual art. It requires square sheets of paper, which are formed into sculptures of animals or other objects by the process of folding. Contained in this book are twenty-five origami animals I have designed.

Origami can be folded from almost any paper, but is most attractive when made from special paper called origami paper. Origami paper is square and usually comes in packets of assorted sizes and colors. It may be found in many variety and hobby stores, or may be ordered by mail from the Origami Center (31 Union Square West, New York City 10003). Difficult projects are easier to fold if you use the larger sizes of paper. The back side of each sheet of origami paper is white. In this book the colored side of the paper is indicated by the shaded areas.

It is important that you follow the directions carefully. The standard folds, from which most of the animals are created, are explained in detail at the beginning of the book. I have used the Randlett-Yoshizawa method of notation to indicate the folds. The folding procedures become increasingly difficult as you progress in the text, so it is suggested that you familiarize yourself with the earlier projects first.

The following rules should help guide you through the metamorphosis of folding. Examine step one; if there are any creased-folds in the square, fold them first. Make all further folds according to the instructions provided by lines, arrows and captions. Be aware of the instructions in the next step so that you know what each fold will become. Fold slowly and accurately and crease each fold with your fingernail to keep the folds crisp.

I would like to thank my brothers, Andy and Mark Montroll, for taking the photographs that appear at the beginning of each project. I would also like to thank Judy Rubenstein and Sheldon Cohn for the front cover picture.

It is my hope that you will enjoy making my origami menagerie.

CONTENTS

SYMBOLS

— — — — —   Valley-fold.

— — ·· — — ·· — — · — —   Mountain-fold.

————————   Creased-fold. Fold and unfold beforehand; or existing fold.

· · · · · · · · · · · · · · · ·   X-ray view or guidelines.

Fold in direction of arrow.

Fold behind.

Unfold.

Fold and unfold.

Push in, sink, squash or reverse-fold.

Turn model over.

Fold and fold again.

Pleat-fold, combination of mountain- and valley-folds.

BASIC FOLDS AND BASES

Pleat-fold

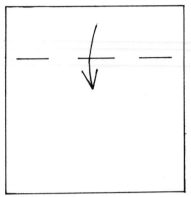

Valley-fold. Fold forward.

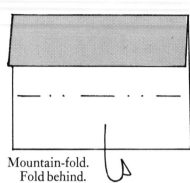

Mountain-fold.
Fold behind.

Finished model displaying both folds.

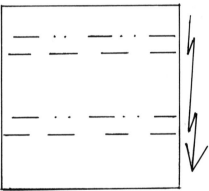

Combination of mountain- and
valley-folds.

PLEAT-FOLD

Kite-fold

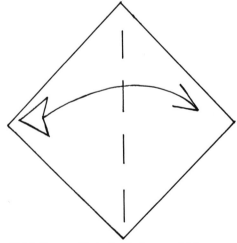

Fold diagonally in half, then unfold.

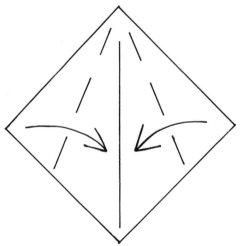

Valley-fold along lines to center crease.

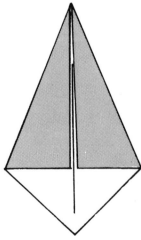

KITE-FOLD

Reverse-and Crimp-folds

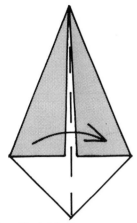

1. To fold all reverse- and crimp-folds begin with kite-fold and fold in half.

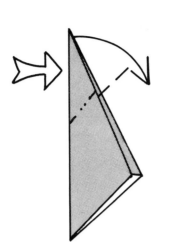
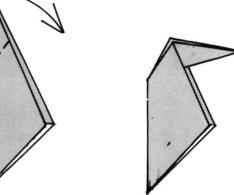

2. Fold tip between outer layers. (This fold will appear both ways in future diagrams.)

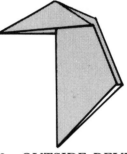

3. INSIDE REVERSE-FOLD

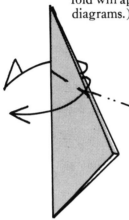

2. Open model slightly, then fold tip around outer layers.

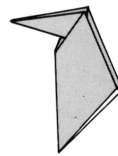

3. OUTSIDE REVERSE-FOLD

2. Fold behind two reverse-folds, simultaneously.

3. INSIDE CRIMP-FOLD I

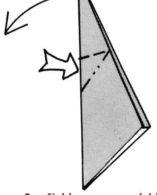

2. Fold one reverse-fold to right, then one to left.

3. INSIDE CRIMP-FOLD II

2. Fold one reverse-fold in front and one behind.

3. THE OUTSIDE CRIMP-FOLD

Rabbit Ear

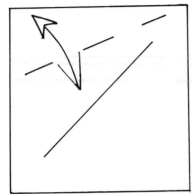

1. Fold and unfold diagonally in half. Fold one side to the center as in a kite-fold and unfold.

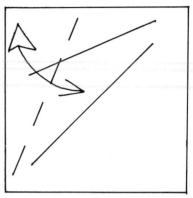

2. Fold and unfold opposite side to the center.

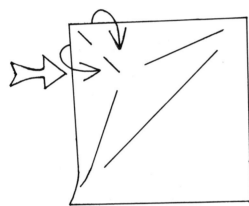

3a. Pinch together sides at the corner and fold down along creases as shown.

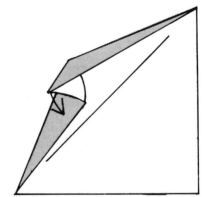

3b. Appearance just before completion.

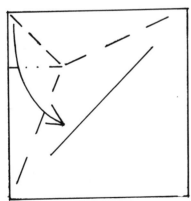

Synopsis of steps 1–3b.

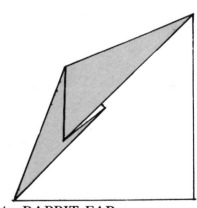

4. RABBIT EAR

Fish Base

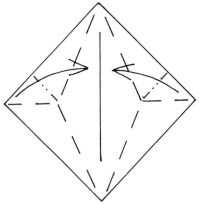
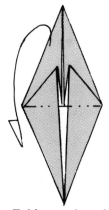

1. Fold two rabbit ears.

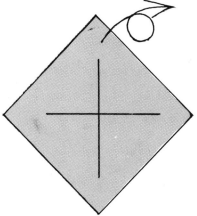
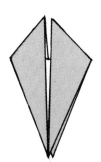

2. Fold upper layer behind.

3. **FISH BASE**

Preliminary-fold

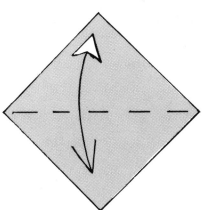

1. Fold diagonally in half, then unfold.

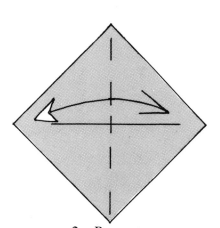

2. Repeat.

3. Turn over model, then turn clockwise.

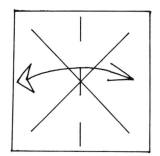

4. Fold in half, then unfold.

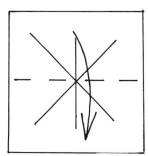

5. Fold in half.

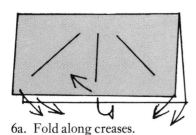

6a. Fold along creases.

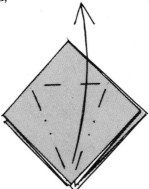

6b. Appearance just before completion.

Synopsis of steps 1-6b.

7. PRELIMINARY-FOLD

Petal-fold I

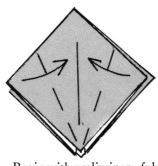

1. Begin with preliminary-fold, then kite-fold.

2. Fold triangular tip down.

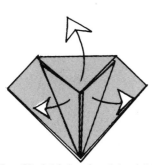

3. Unfold tip, then kite-fold.

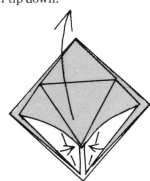

4a. Lift top layer up along creases.

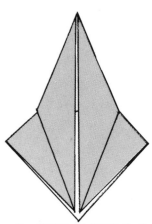

4b. Fold along creases while lifting.

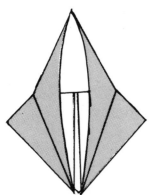

4c. Appearance just before completion.

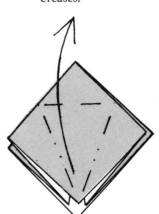

Synopsis of steps 1–4c.

5. PETAL-FOLD I

Bird Base

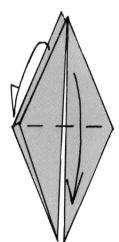

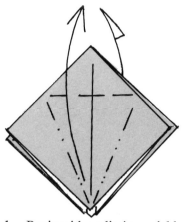

1. Begin with preliminary-fold, then petal-fold both sides.

2. Fold tops of both sides down.

3. **BIRD BASE**

Squash-fold

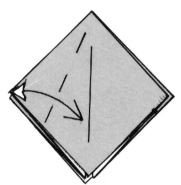

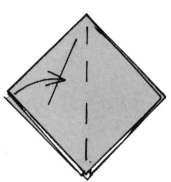

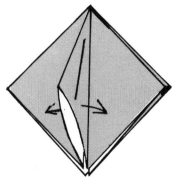

1. Begin with preliminary-fold, then fold and unfold as shown.

2. Lift flap out from sheet.

3. Insert finger inside flap to squash it.

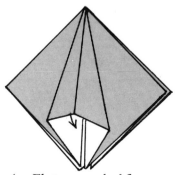

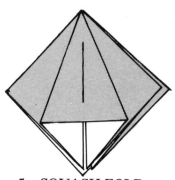

4. Flatten squashed flap.

5. **SQUASH-FOLD**

Petal-fold II

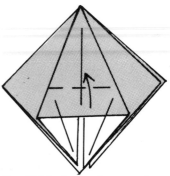

1. Begin with preliminary-fold, squash-fold one layer. Fold and unfold the kite-fold.

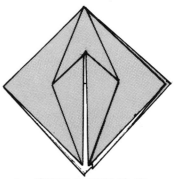

2. Fold edge up into a point.

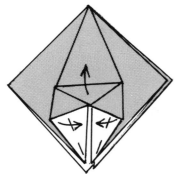

3. Fold along edges.

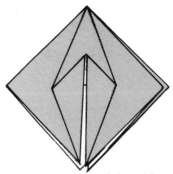

4. **PETAL-FOLD II**

Frog Base

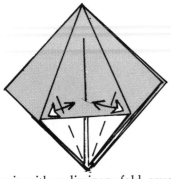

1. Begin with petal-fold II.

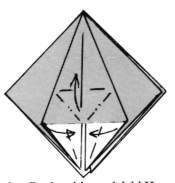

2. Repeat on remaining sides.

3. **FROG BASE**

Stretched Bird Base

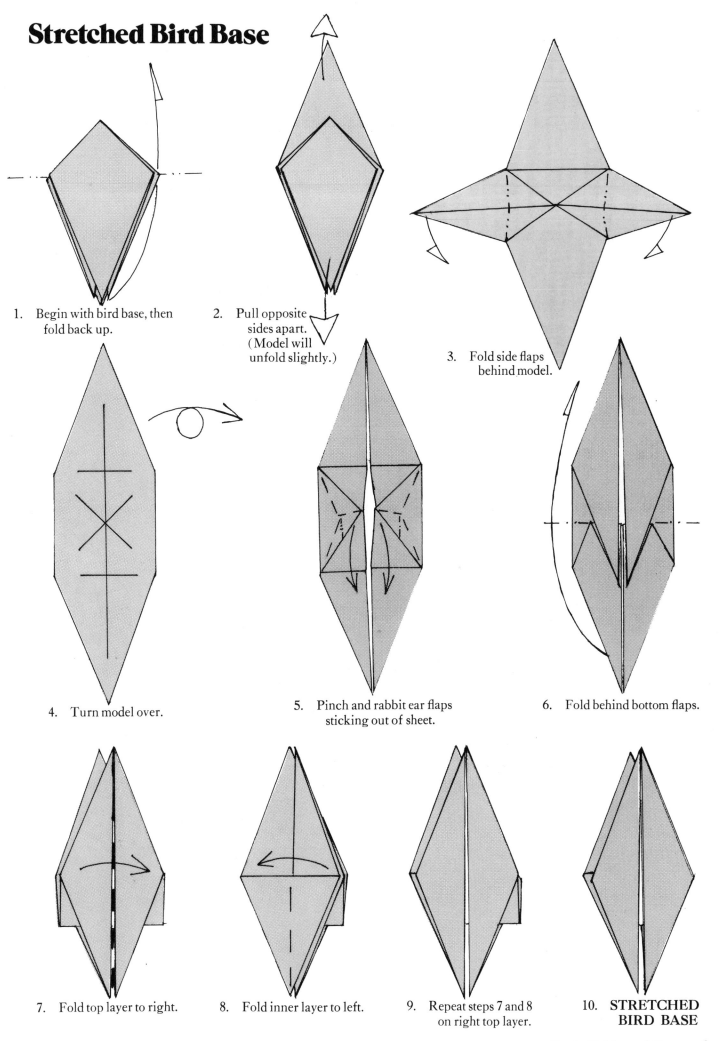

1. Begin with bird base, then fold back up.

2. Pull opposite sides apart. (Model will unfold slightly.)

3. Fold side flaps behind model.

4. Turn model over.

5. Pinch and rabbit ear flaps sticking out of sheet.

6. Fold behind bottom flaps.

7. Fold top layer to right.

8. Fold inner layer to left.

9. Repeat steps 7 and 8 on right top layer.

10. **STRETCHED BIRD BASE**

Water Bomb Base

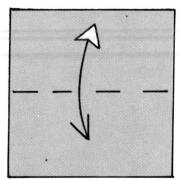

1. Fold horizontally in half, then unfold.

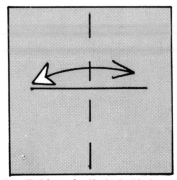

2. Fold vertically in half, then unfold.

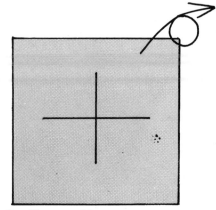

3. Turn model over.

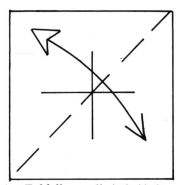

4. Fold diagonally in half, then unfold.

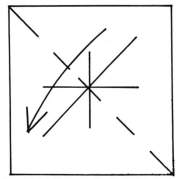

5. Fold diagonally in half along dashed line.

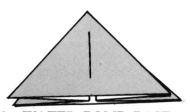

6. Fold along creases (Model will open slightly.)

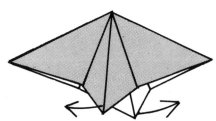

7. Fold along creases.

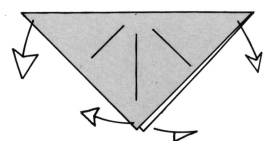

8. WATER BOMB BASE

Double Rabbit Ear

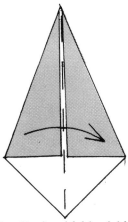

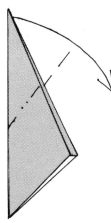

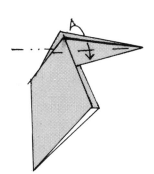

1. Begin with kite-fold, then fold in half.

2. Inside reverse-fold.

3. Fold each flap in half.

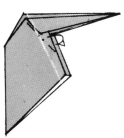

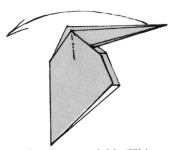

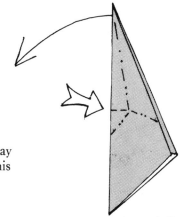

4. Fold base of point behind.

5. Reverse-fold. (This step may be omitted to produce this alternate form.)

6. **DOUBLE RABBIT EAR**

Synopsis of steps 1–5.

Blintz-fold

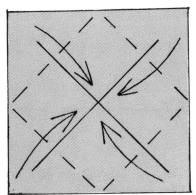

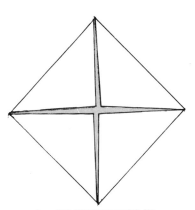

1. Fold and unfold diagonally in half to form creases as shown, then fold four corners to center.

2. **BLINTZ-FOLD**

Blintz Bird Base

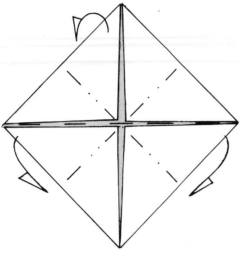

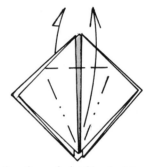

1. Begin with blintz-fold, then preliminary-fold back.

2. Squash-fold both sides. Fold tips up.

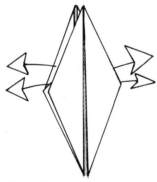

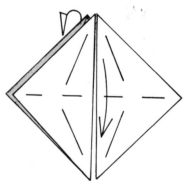

3. Pull out four corners of original square.

4. Fold both sides in half.

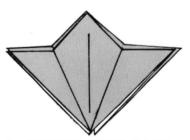

5. BLINTZ BIRD BASE

Blintz Frog Base

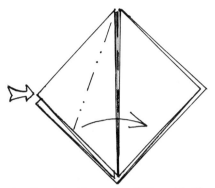

1. Begin with step 1 of blintz-bird base, then squash-fold as shown.

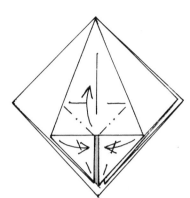

2. Petal-fold.

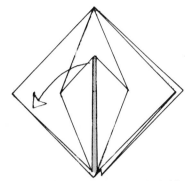

3. Unfold petal- and squash-folds.

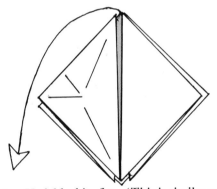

4. Unfold white flap. (This is similar to an outside reverse-fold.)

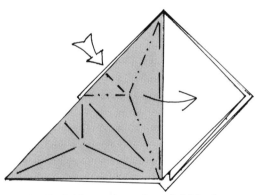

5. Refold squash- and petal-folds along creases as shown.

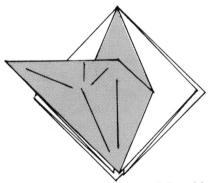

6. Repeat steps 1–5 on remaining sides.

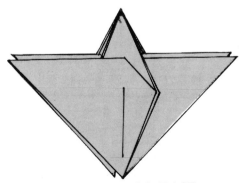

7. **BLINTZ FROG BASE**

FISH

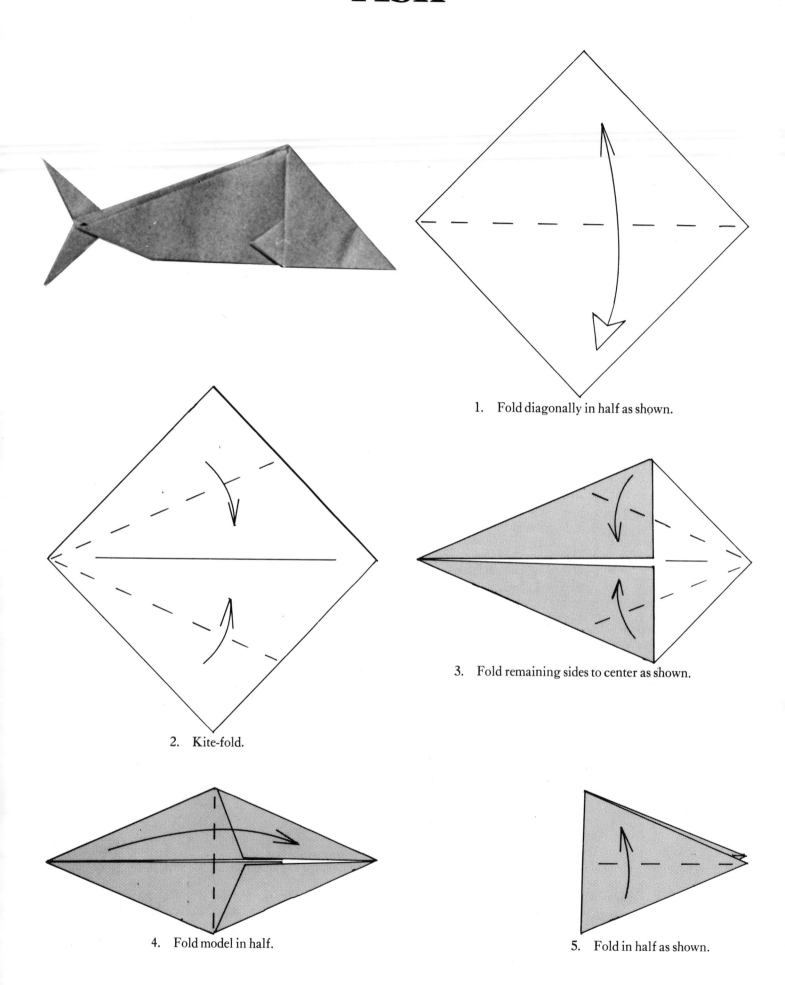

1. Fold diagonally in half as shown.

2. Kite-fold.

3. Fold remaining sides to center as shown.

4. Fold model in half.

5. Fold in half as shown.

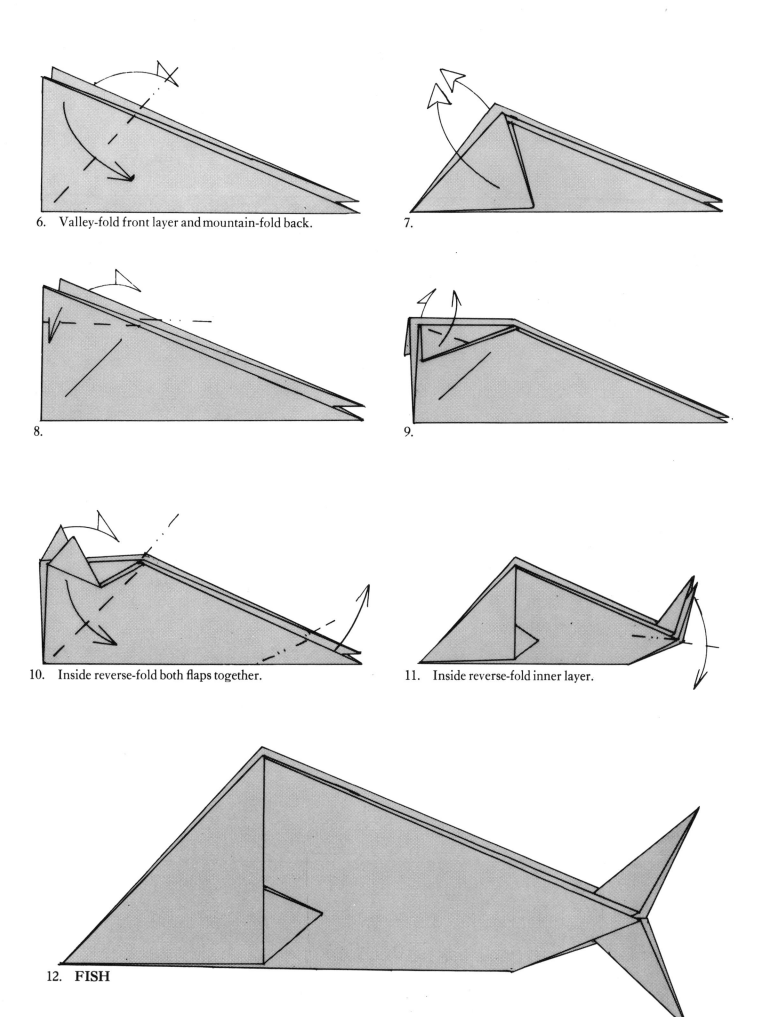

6. Valley-fold front layer and mountain-fold back.

7.

8.

9.

10. Inside reverse-fold both flaps together.

11. Inside reverse-fold inner layer.

12. **FISH**

GOLDFISH

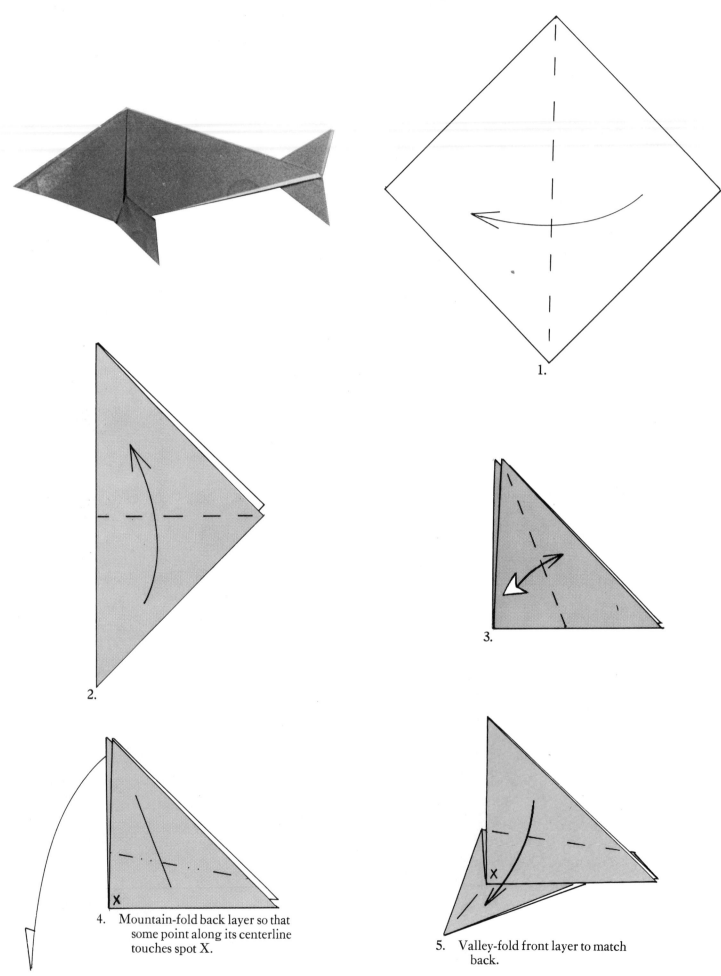

1.

2.

3.

4. Mountain-fold back layer so that some point along its centerline touches spot X.

5. Valley-fold front layer to match back.

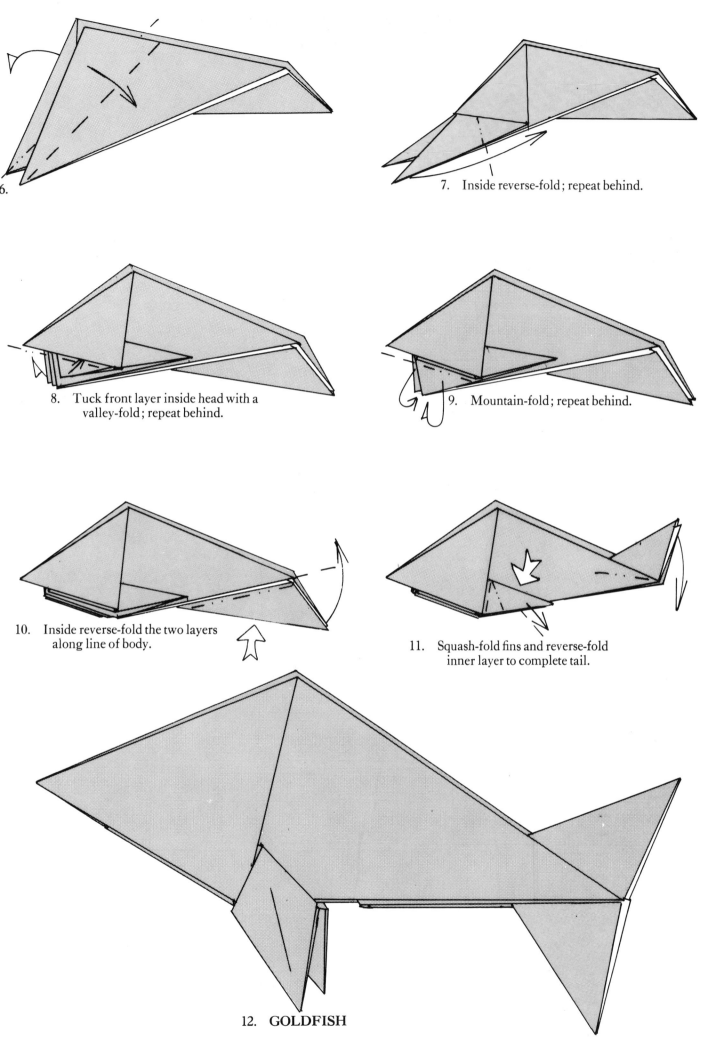

6.

7. Inside reverse-fold; repeat behind.

8. Tuck front layer inside head with a valley-fold; repeat behind.

9. Mountain-fold; repeat behind.

10. Inside reverse-fold the two layers along line of body.

11. Squash-fold fins and reverse-fold inner layer to complete tail.

12. **GOLDFISH**

SEA HORSE

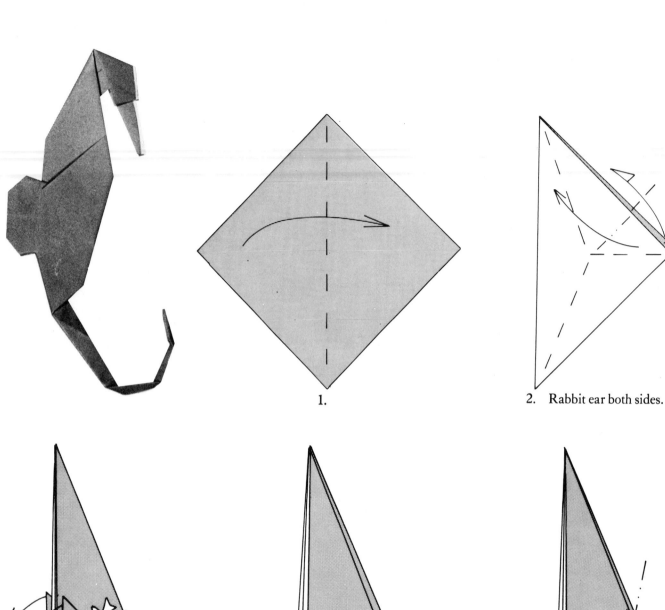

1.

2. Rabbit ear both sides.

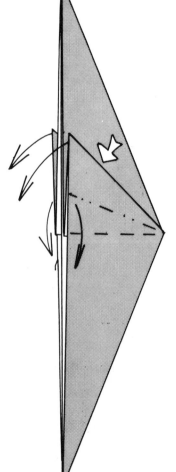

3. Squash-fold each side.

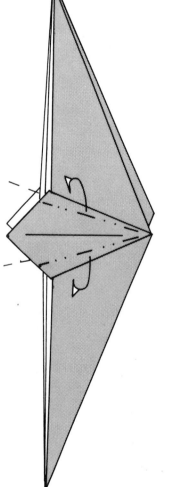

4. Fold some paper behind; repeat on back.

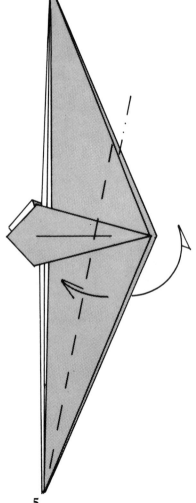

5.

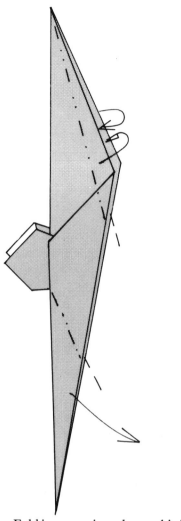

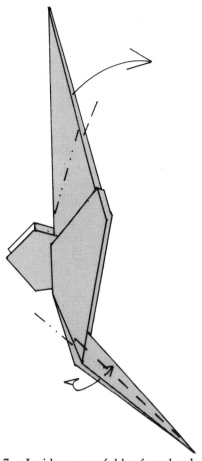

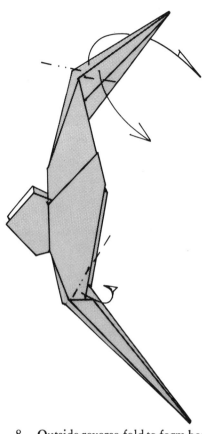

6. Fold in approximately one third of side. Inside reverse-fold to form tail.

7. Inside reverse-fold to form head. Fold outside half of tail; repeat behind.

8. Outside reverse-fold to form head. Fold base of tail inside.

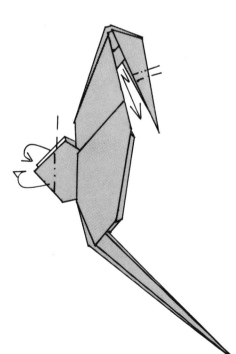

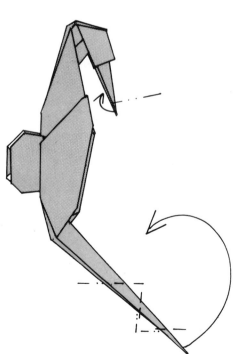

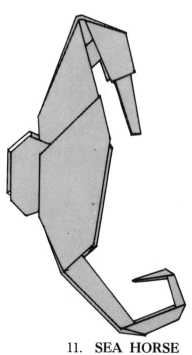

11. **SEA HORSE**

9. Inside crimp-fold. Fold tips of fin inside.

10. Reverse-fold tip inside nose. Curl tail with series of reverse-folds.

WHALE

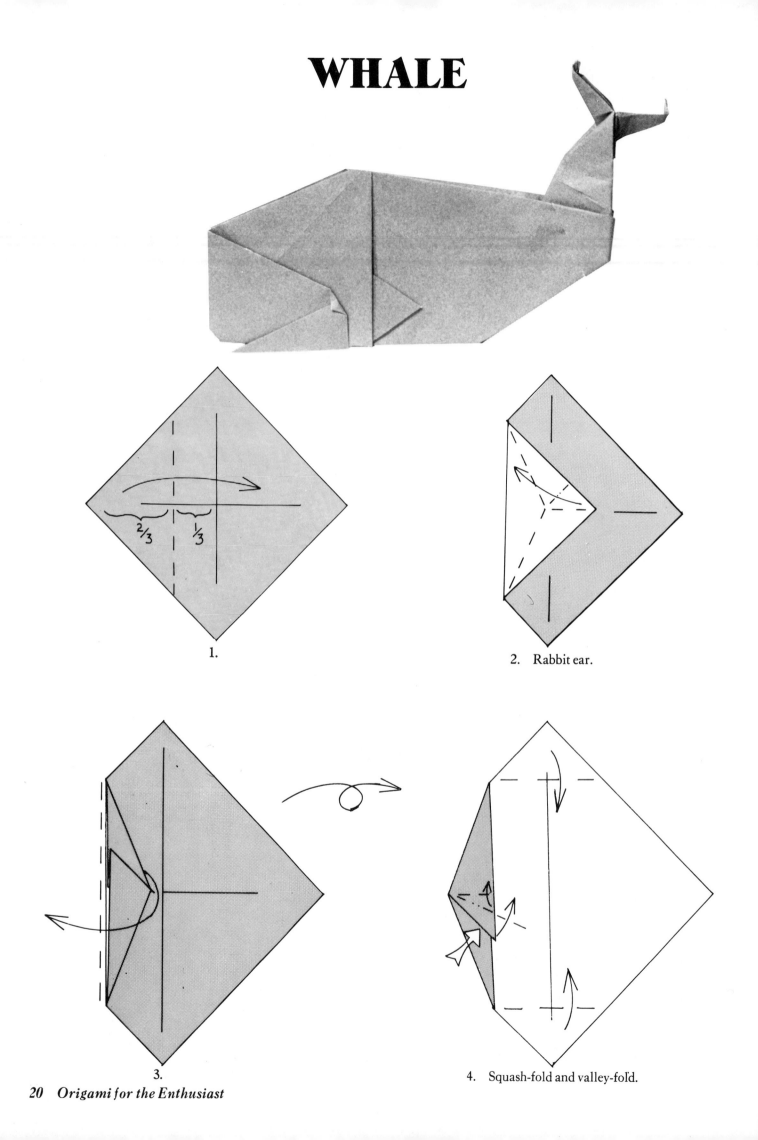

1.

2. Rabbit ear.

3.

4. Squash-fold and valley-fold.

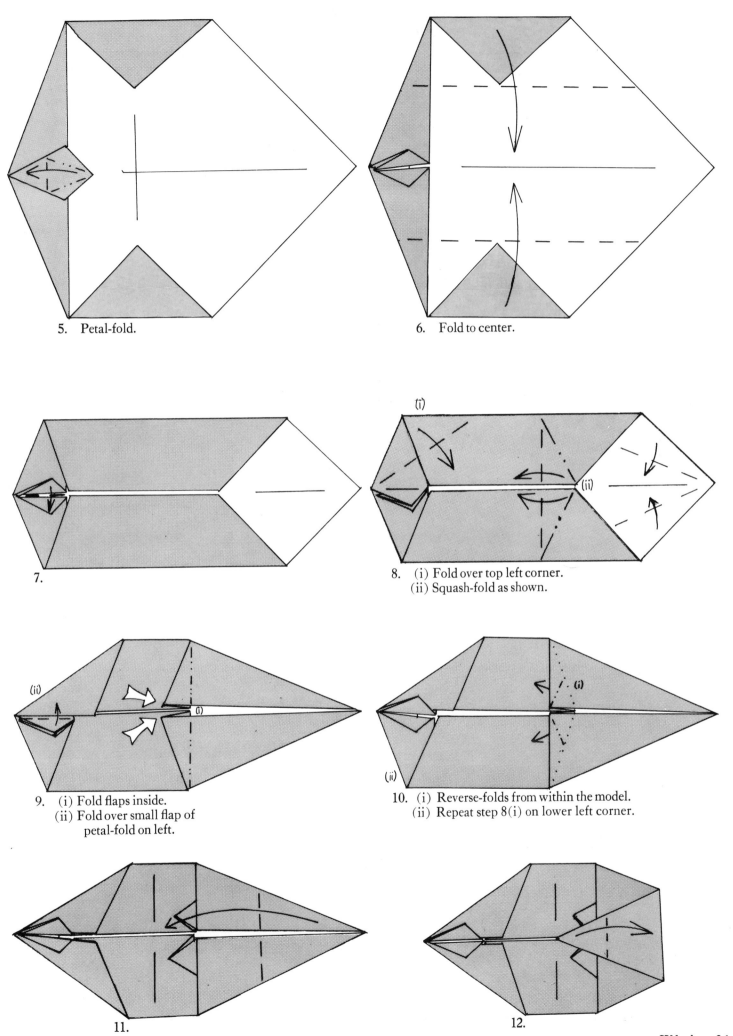

5. Petal-fold.

6. Fold to center.

7.

8. (i) Fold over top left corner.
   (ii) Squash-fold as shown.

9. (i) Fold flaps inside.
   (ii) Fold over small flap of
        petal-fold on left.

10. (i) Reverse-folds from within the model.
    (ii) Repeat step 8(i) on lower left corner.

11.

12.

Whale 21

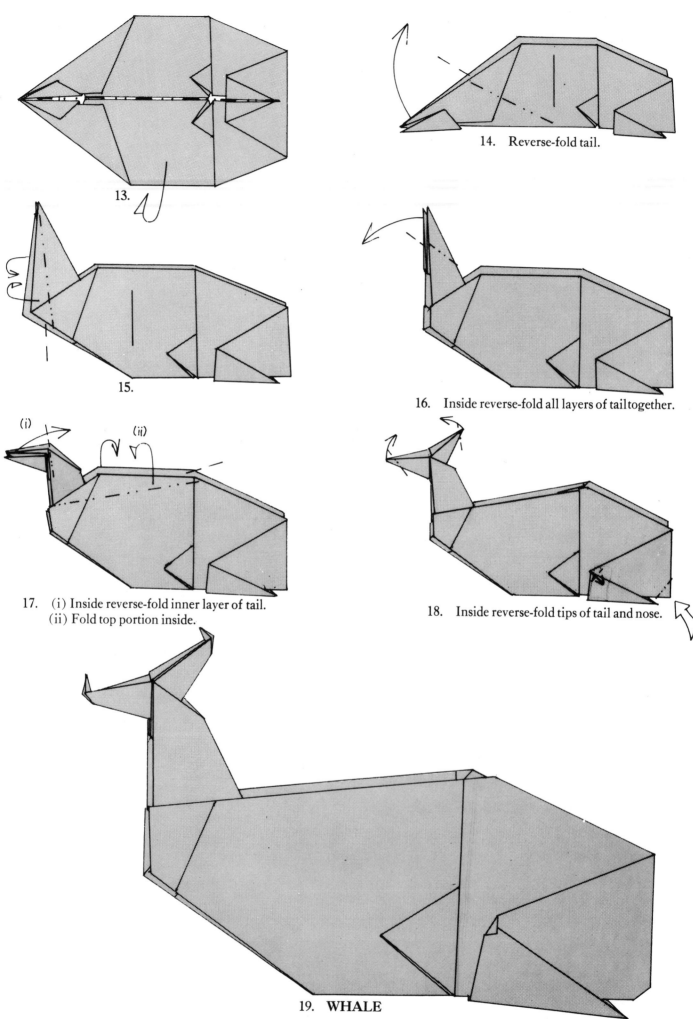

13.

14. Reverse-fold tail.

15.

16. Inside reverse-fold all layers of tail together.

17. (i) Inside reverse-fold inner layer of tail.
(ii) Fold top portion inside.

18. Inside reverse-fold tips of tail and nose.

19. **WHALE**

SUNFISH

1.

2.

3. If spot X does not touch center of sheet, adjust first two folds.

4. Squash-fold to finish rabbit ear.

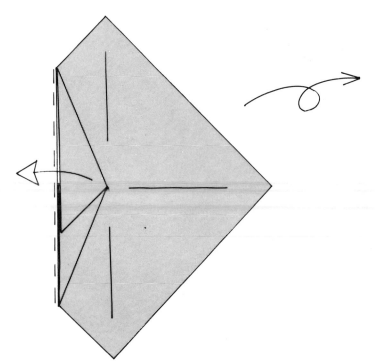

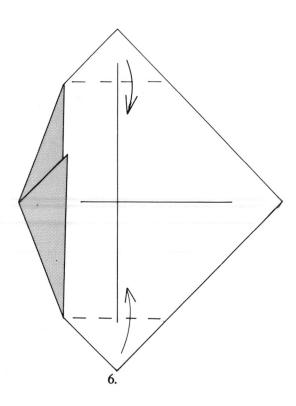

5. Unfold along dashed line only.
   Turn model over.

6.

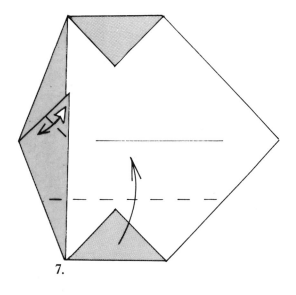

7.

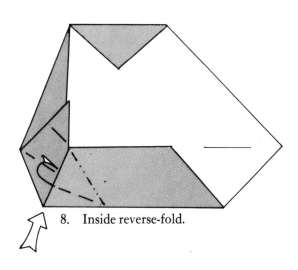

8. Inside reverse-fold.

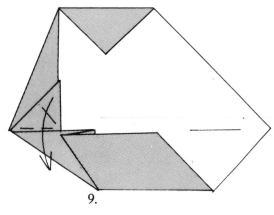

9.

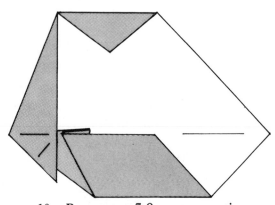

10. Repeat steps 7–9 on upper portion.

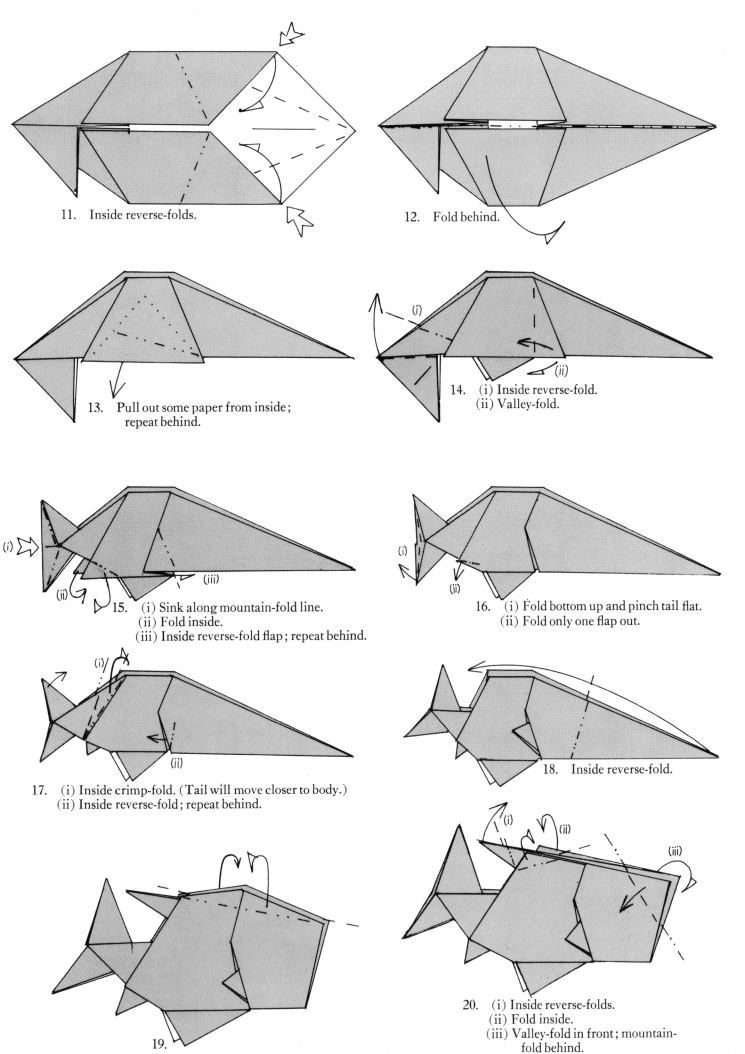

11. Inside reverse-folds.

12. Fold behind.

13. Pull out some paper from inside; repeat behind.

14. (i) Inside reverse-fold.
(ii) Valley-fold.

15. (i) Sink along mountain-fold line.
(ii) Fold inside.
(iii) Inside reverse-fold flap; repeat behind.

16. (i) Fold bottom up and pinch tail flat.
(ii) Fold only one flap out.

17. (i) Inside crimp-fold. (Tail will move closer to body.)
(ii) Inside reverse-fold; repeat behind.

18. Inside reverse-fold.

19.

20. (i) Inside reverse-folds.
(ii) Fold inside.
(iii) Valley-fold in front; mountain-fold behind.

Sunfish 25

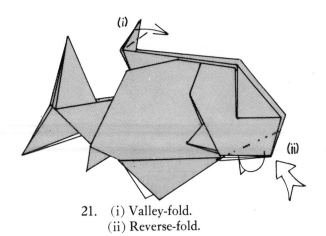

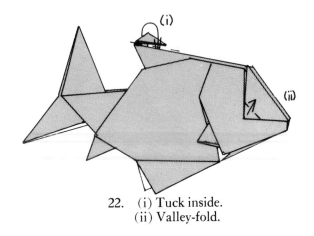

21. (i) Valley-fold.
    (ii) Reverse-fold.

22. (i) Tuck inside.
    (ii) Valley-fold.

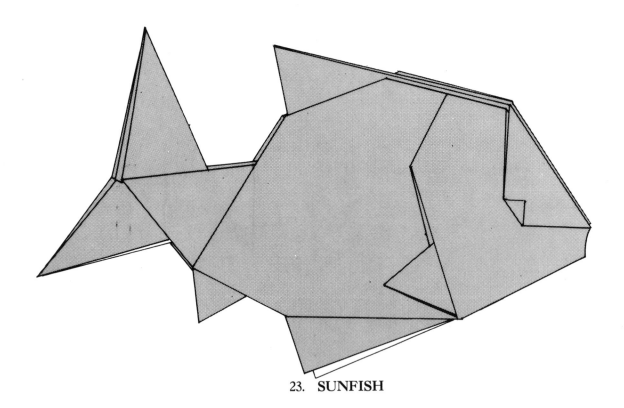

23. **SUNFISH**

VULTURE

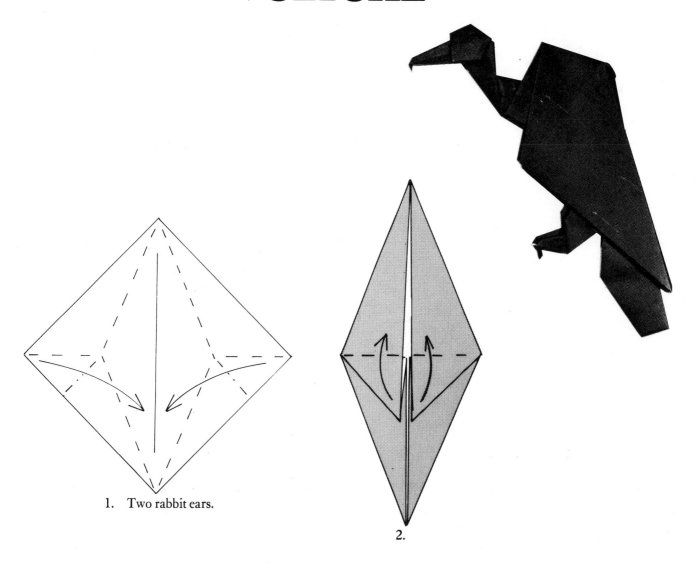

1. Two rabbit ears.

2.

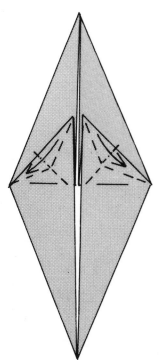

3. Two rabbit ears.

4.

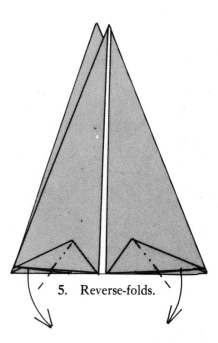

5. Reverse-folds.

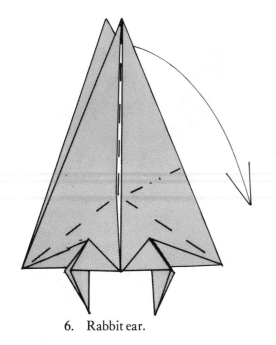

6. Rabbit ear.

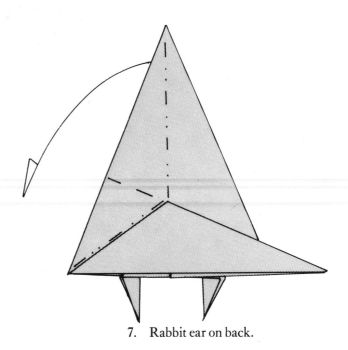

7. Rabbit ear on back.

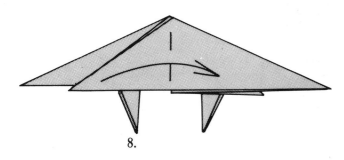

8.

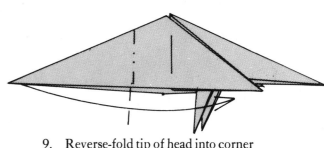

9. Reverse-fold tip of head into corner of top wing.

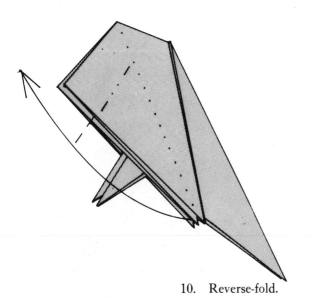

10. Reverse-fold.

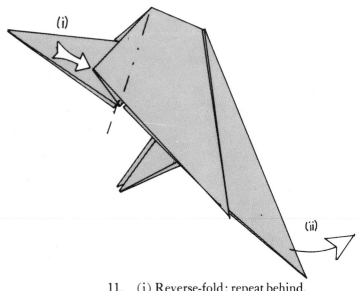

11. (i) Reverse-fold; repeat behind.
(ii) Slide tail out.

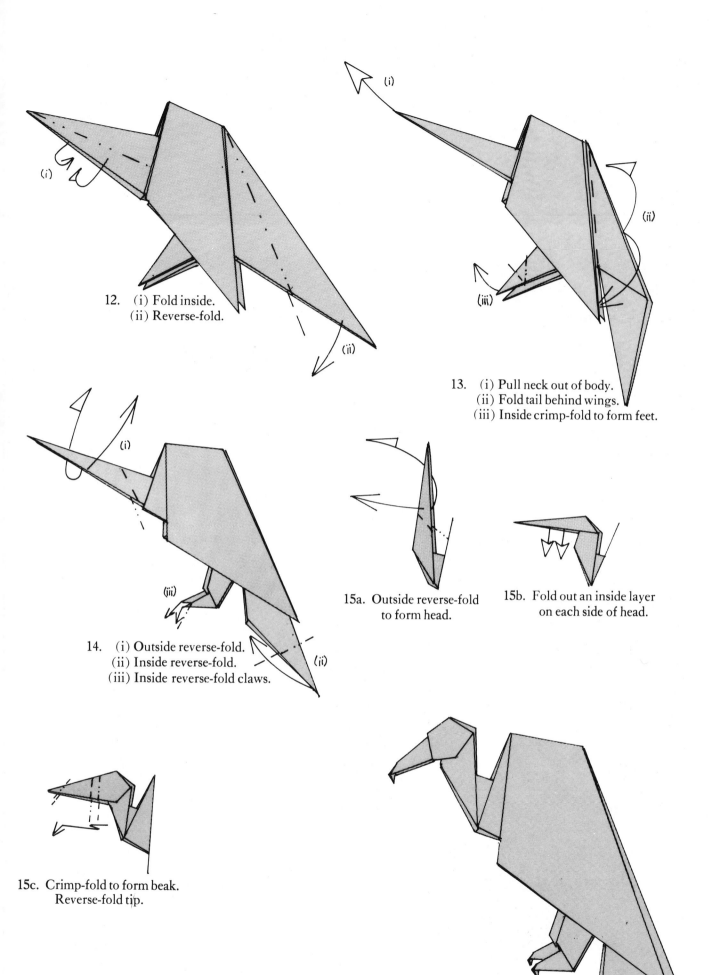

12. (i) Fold inside.
    (ii) Reverse-fold.

13. (i) Pull neck out of body.
    (ii) Fold tail behind wings.
    (iii) Inside crimp-fold to form feet.

14. (i) Outside reverse-fold.
    (ii) Inside reverse-fold.
    (iii) Inside reverse-fold claws.

15a. Outside reverse-fold
     to form head.

15b. Fold out an inside layer
     on each side of head.

15c. Crimp-fold to form beak.
     Reverse-fold tip.

16. **VULTURE**

OSTRICH

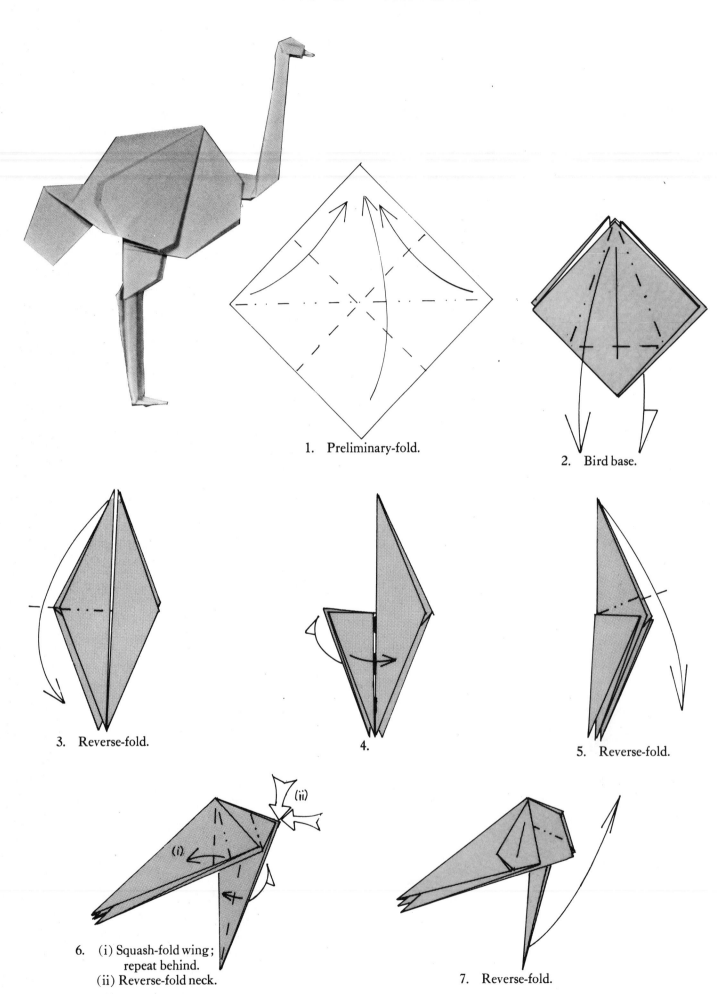

1. Preliminary-fold.

2. Bird base.

3. Reverse-fold.

4.

5. Reverse-fold.

6. (i) Squash-fold wing;
   repeat behind.
   (ii) Reverse-fold neck.

7. Reverse-fold.

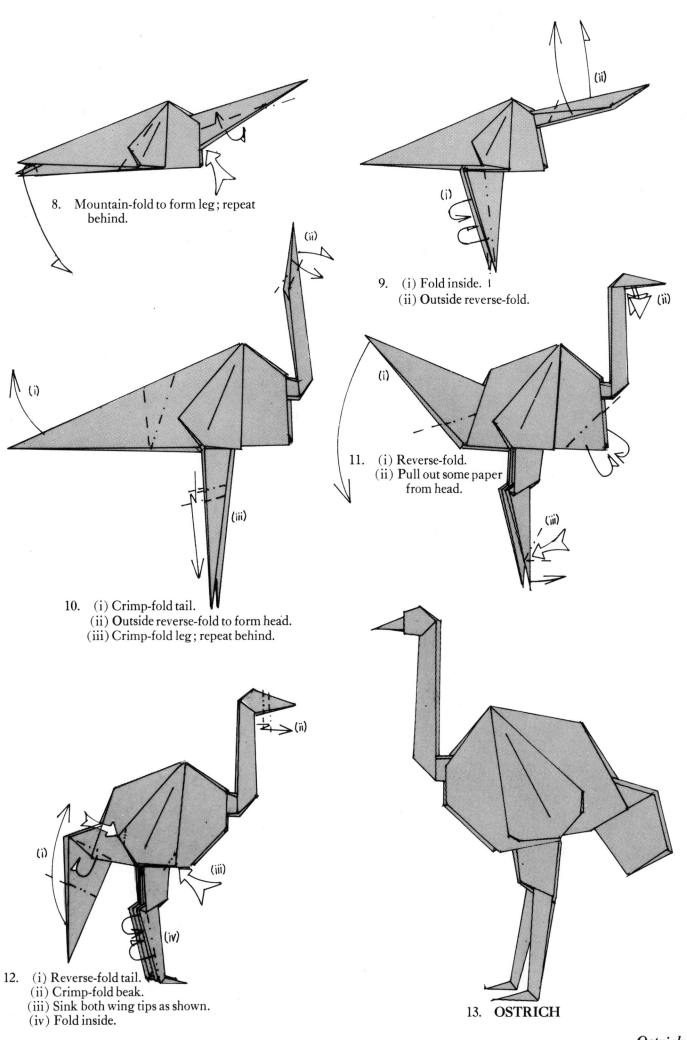

8. Mountain-fold to form leg; repeat behind.

9. (i) Fold inside.
   (ii) Outside reverse-fold.

10. (i) Crimp-fold tail.
    (ii) Outside reverse-fold to form head.
    (iii) Crimp-fold leg; repeat behind.

11. (i) Reverse-fold.
    (ii) Pull out some paper from head.

12. (i) Reverse-fold tail.
    (ii) Crimp-fold beak.
    (iii) Sink both wing tips as shown.
    (iv) Fold inside.

13. OSTRICH

TOUCAN

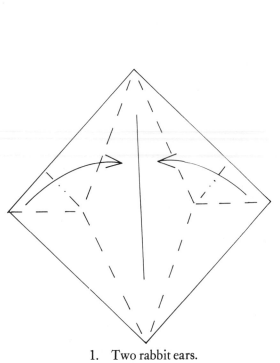

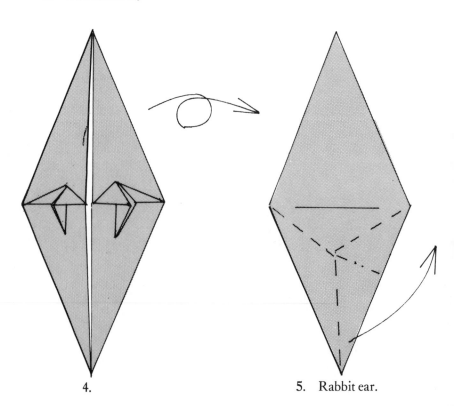

1. Two rabbit ears.

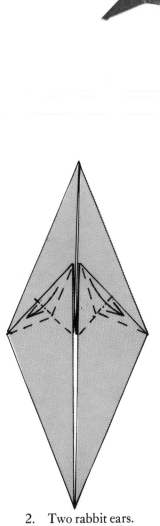

2. Two rabbit ears.

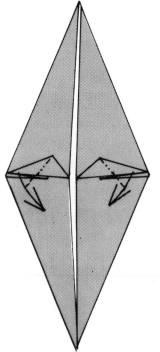

3. Reverse-folds.

4.

5. Rabbit ear.

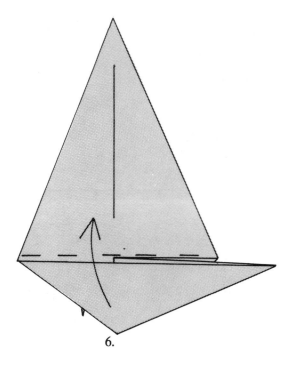

6.

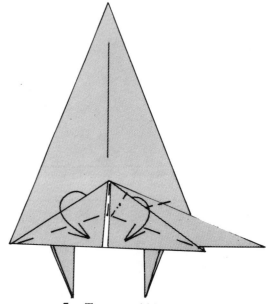

7. Treat as rabbit ear.

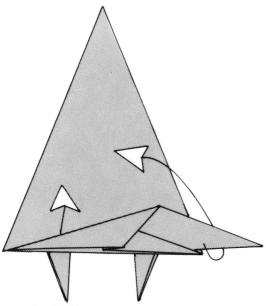

8. Fold up from behind.

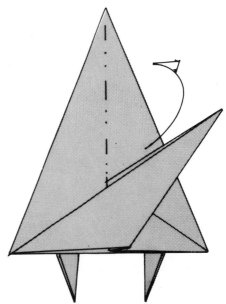

9. Mountain-fold.

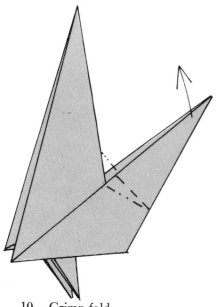

10. Crimp-fold.

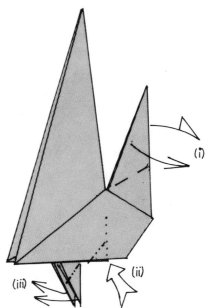

11. (i) Outside reverse-fold.
(ii) Reverse-fold inner layer.
(iii) Inside reverse-fold to form feet.

Toucan 33

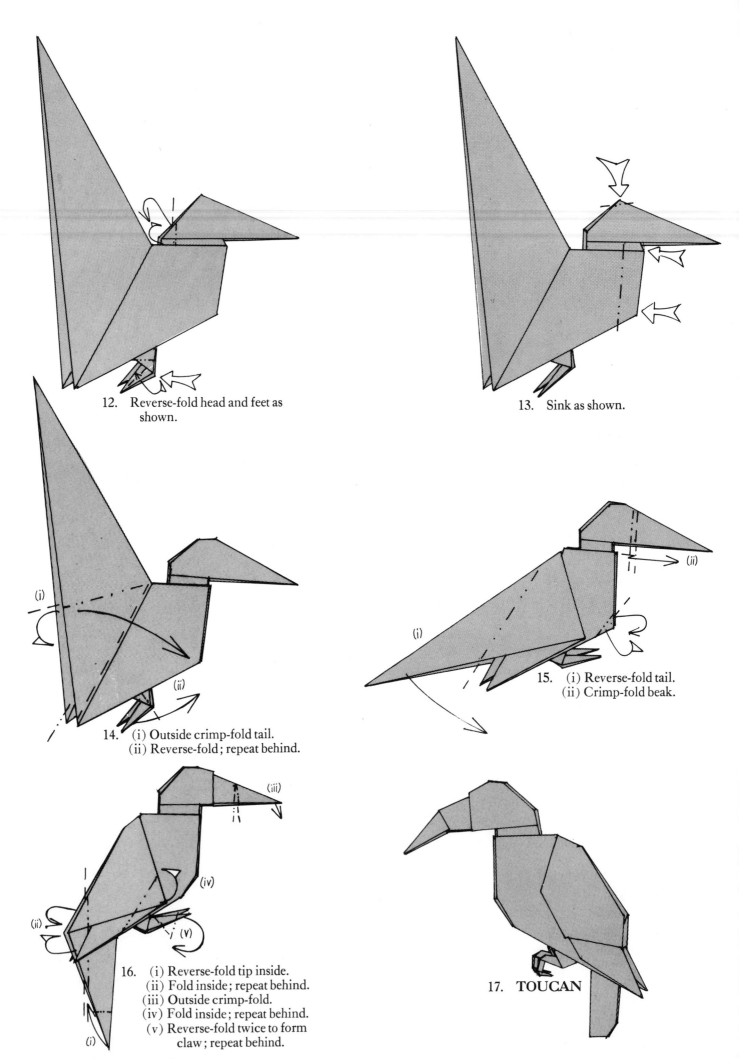

12. Reverse-fold head and feet as shown.

13. Sink as shown.

14. (i) Outside crimp-fold tail.
(ii) Reverse-fold; repeat behind.

15. (i) Reverse-fold tail.
(ii) Crimp-fold beak.

16. (i) Reverse-fold tip inside.
(ii) Fold inside; repeat behind.
(iii) Outside crimp-fold.
(iv) Fold inside; repeat behind.
(v) Reverse-fold twice to form claw; repeat behind.

17. **TOUCAN**

STORK

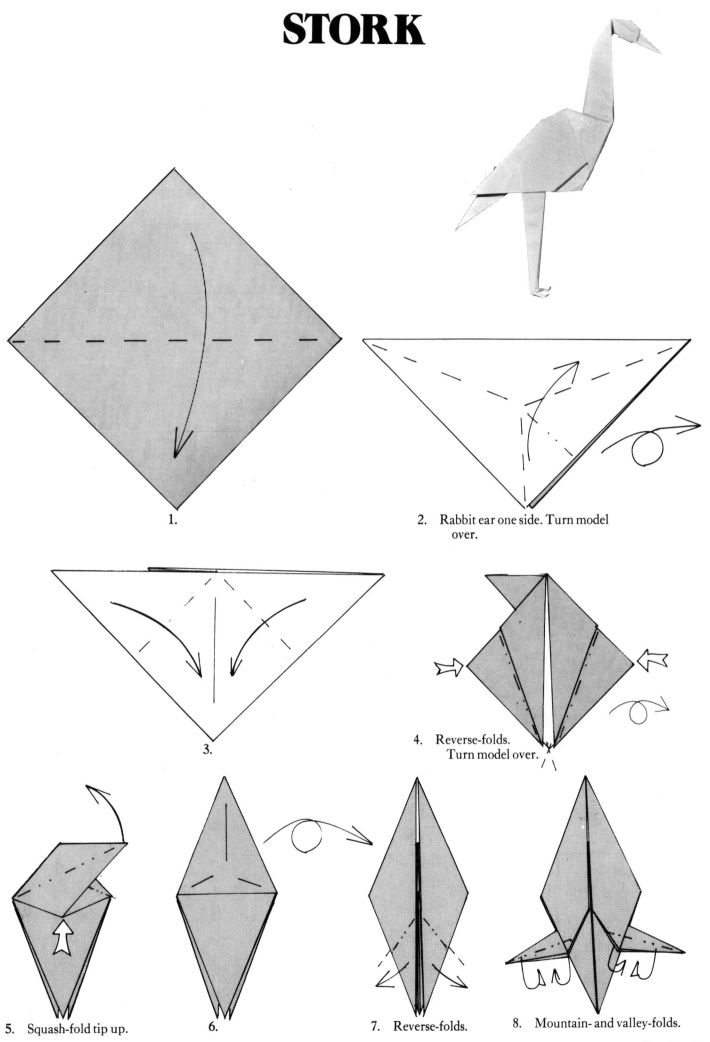

1.

2. Rabbit ear one side. Turn model over.

3.

4. Reverse-folds. Turn model over.

5. Squash-fold tip up.

6.

7. Reverse-folds.

8. Mountain- and valley-folds.

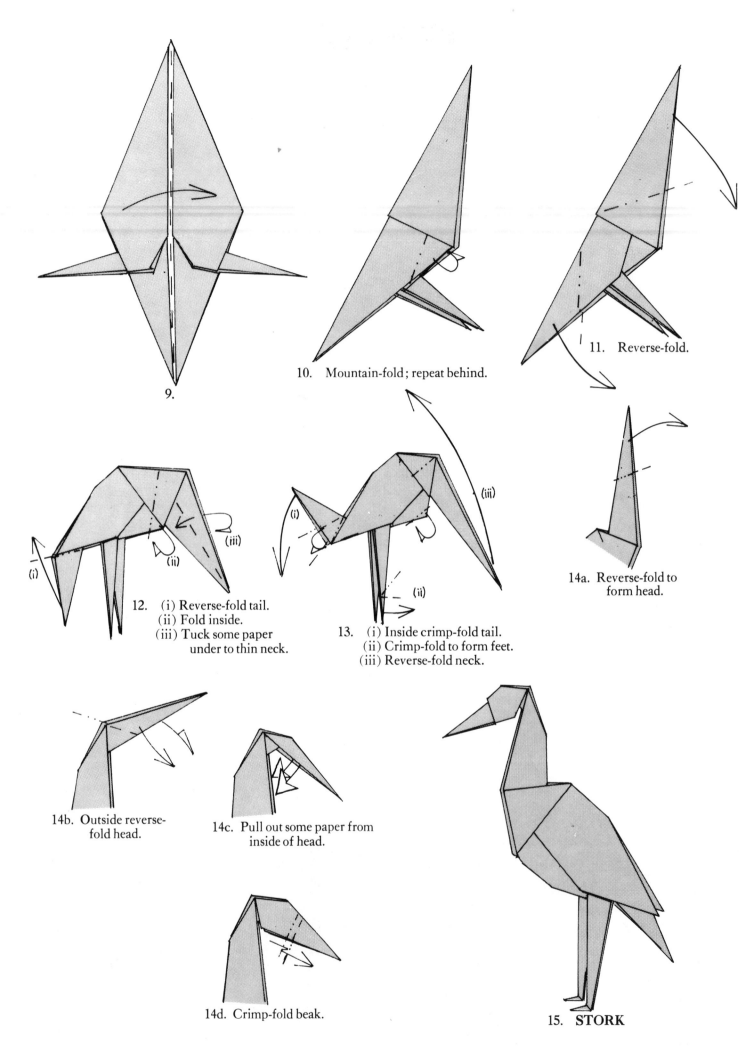

9.

10. Mountain-fold; repeat behind.

11. Reverse-fold.

12. (i) Reverse-fold tail.
     (ii) Fold inside.
     (iii) Tuck some paper
         under to thin neck.

13. (i) Inside crimp-fold tail.
     (ii) Crimp-fold to form feet.
     (iii) Reverse-fold neck.

14a. Reverse-fold to
      form head.

14b. Outside reverse-
      fold head.

14c. Pull out some paper from
      inside of head.

14d. Crimp-fold beak.

15. STORK

GOOSE

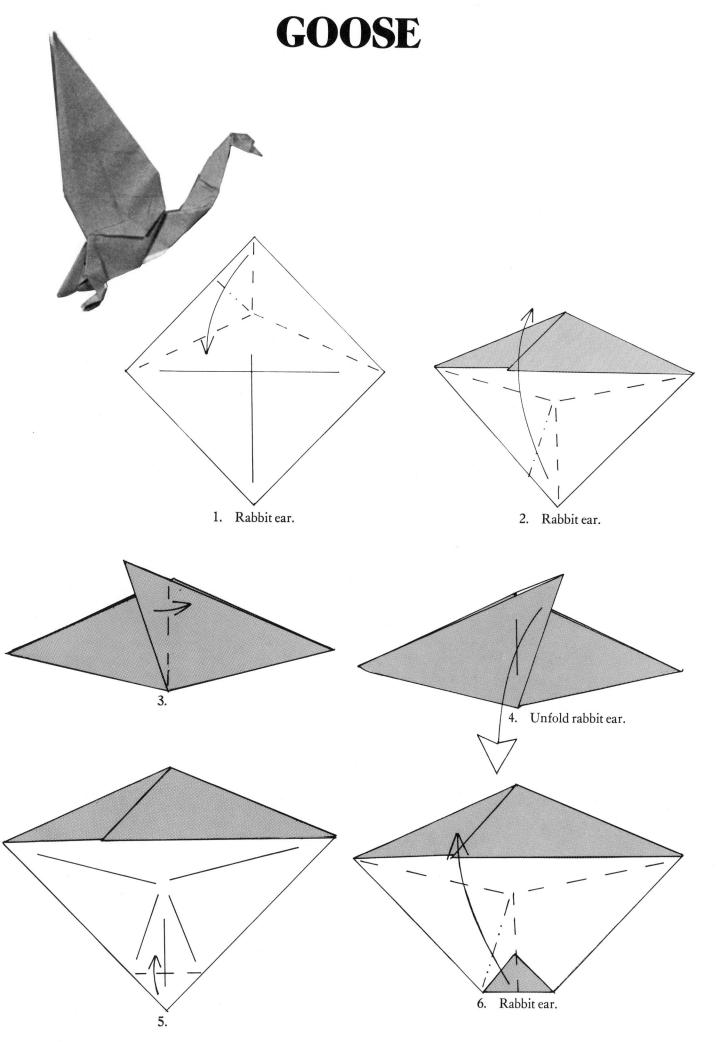

1. Rabbit ear.

2. Rabbit ear.

3.

4. Unfold rabbit ear.

5.

6. Rabbit ear.

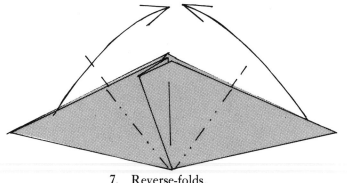

7. Reverse-folds.

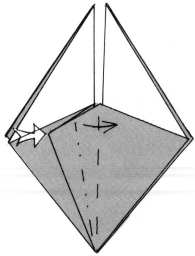

8. Squash-fold.

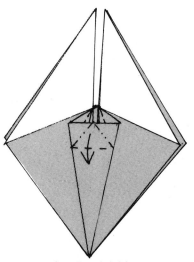

9. Petal-fold.

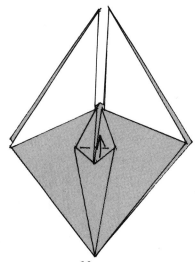

10.

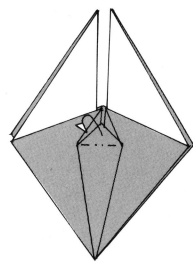

11. Fold flap inside.

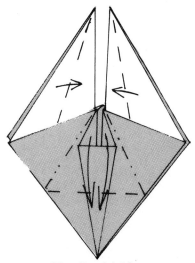

12. Petal-fold.

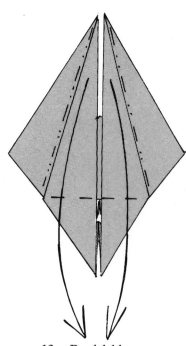

13. Petal-fold.

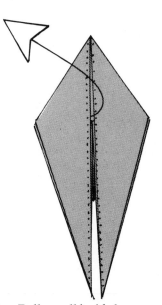

14. Pull out all inside layers attached to sides marked by dotted lines. (These layers correspond to rabbit ear in step 1.)

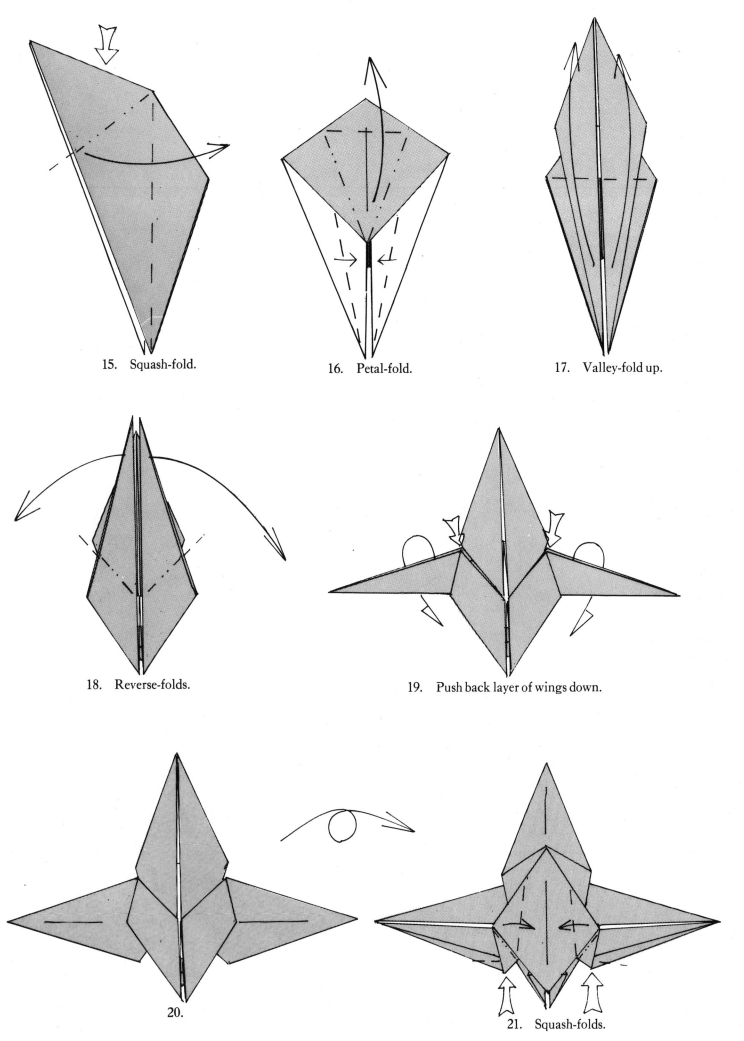

15.   Squash-fold.

16.   Petal-fold.

17.   Valley-fold up.

18.   Reverse-folds.

19.   Push back layer of wings down.

20.

21.   Squash-folds.

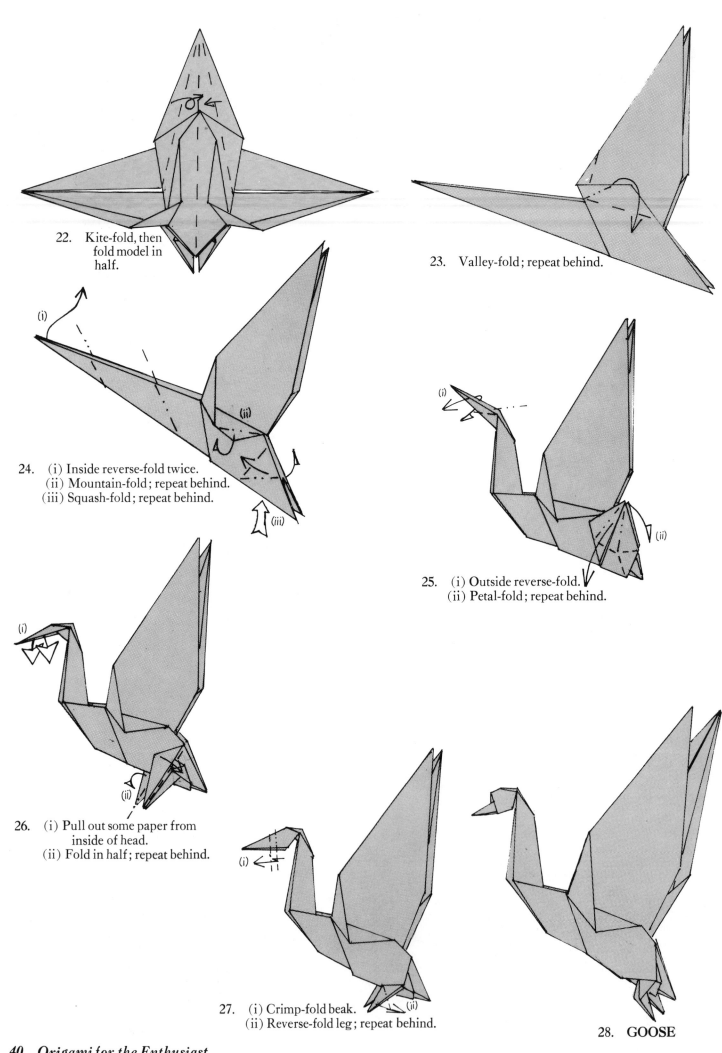

22. Kite-fold, then fold model in half.

23. Valley-fold; repeat behind.

24. (i) Inside reverse-fold twice.
    (ii) Mountain-fold; repeat behind.
    (iii) Squash-fold; repeat behind.

25. (i) Outside reverse-fold.
    (ii) Petal-fold; repeat behind.

26. (i) Pull out some paper from inside of head.
    (ii) Fold in half; repeat behind.

27. (i) Crimp-fold beak.
    (ii) Reverse-fold leg; repeat behind.

28. **GOOSE**

ROBIN

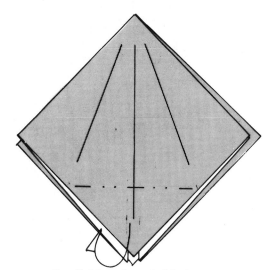

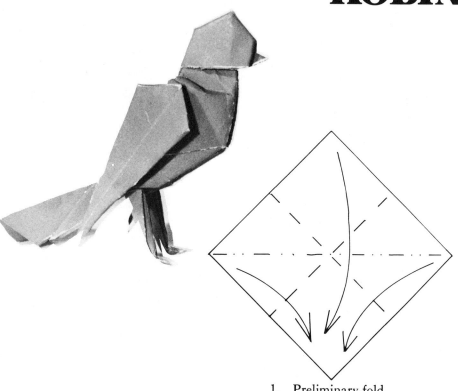

1. Preliminary-fold.

2. Kite-fold each side, then unfold.

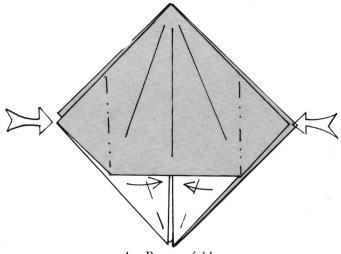

3. Fold top layer behind.

4. Reverse-folds.

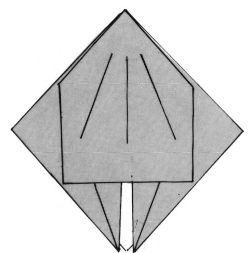

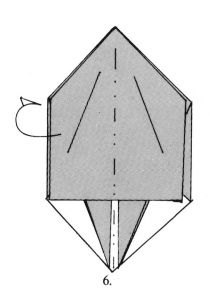

5. Repeat step 4 behind.

6.

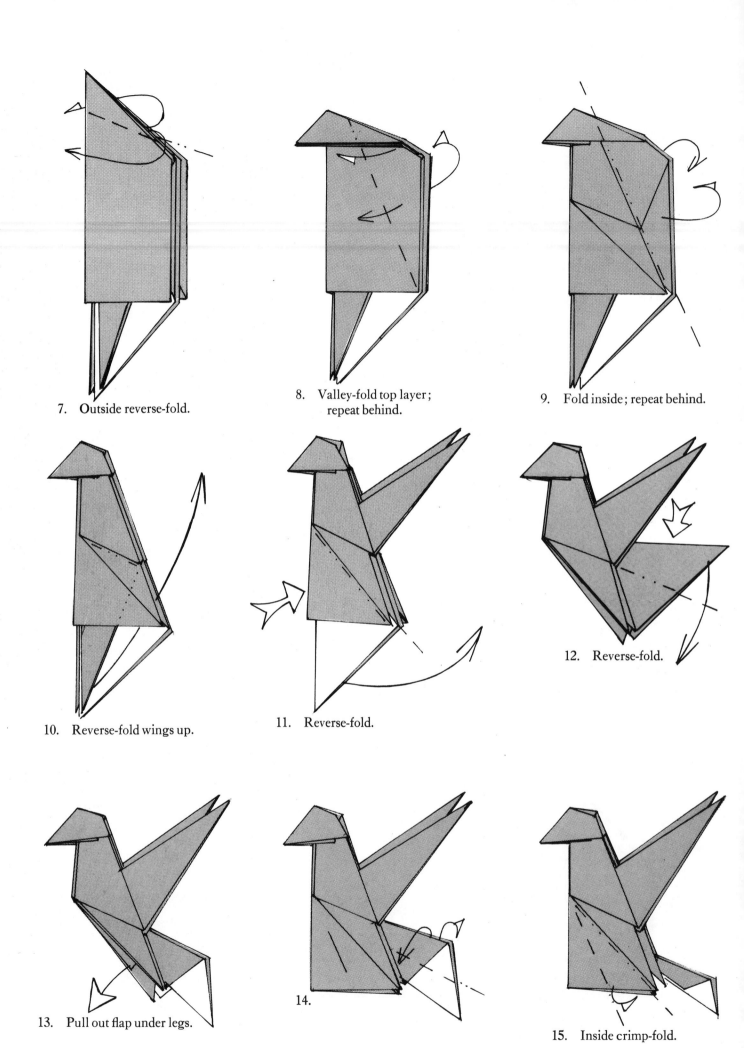

7. Outside reverse-fold.

8. Valley-fold top layer; repeat behind.

9. Fold inside; repeat behind.

10. Reverse-fold wings up.

11. Reverse-fold.

12. Reverse-fold.

13. Pull out flap under legs.

14.

15. Inside crimp-fold.

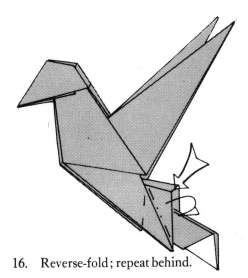

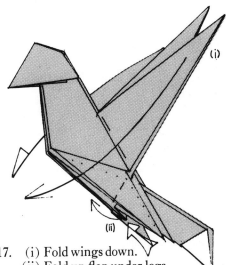

16. Reverse-fold; repeat behind.

17. (i) Fold wings down.
    (ii) Fold up flap under legs.

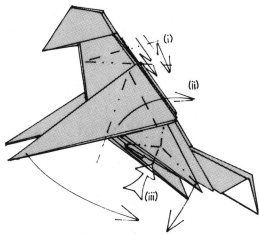

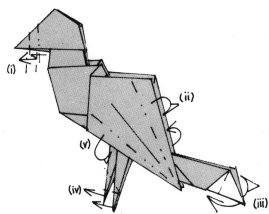

18. (i) Inside crimp-fold neck.
    (ii) Squash-fold wings.
    (iii) Double rabbit ear the legs.

19. (i) Crimp-fold beak.
    (ii) Fold inside.
    (iii) Outside reverse-fold tail.
    (iv) Crimp-fold feet.
    (v) Fold inside.

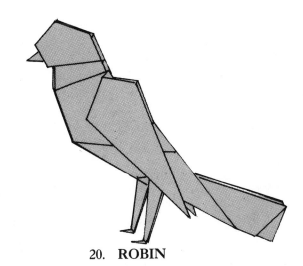

20. **ROBIN**

PEACOCK

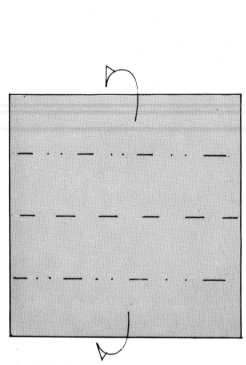

1. Pleat-fold into quarters.

2. Reverse-fold; repeat behind.

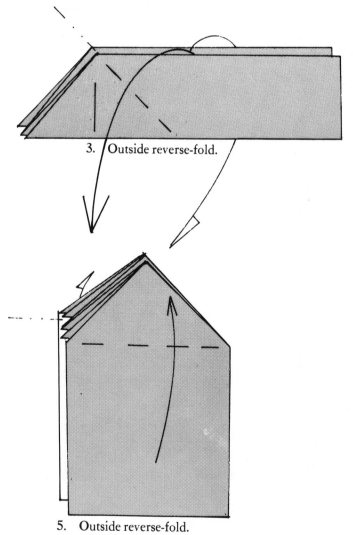

3. Outside reverse-fold.

4. Pull out inner layers.

5. Outside reverse-fold.

6. Valley-fold top layer; repeat behind.

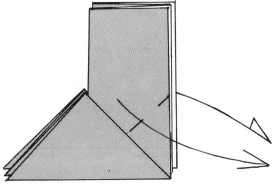

7. Outside reverse-fold.

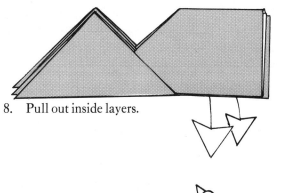

8. Pull out inside layers.

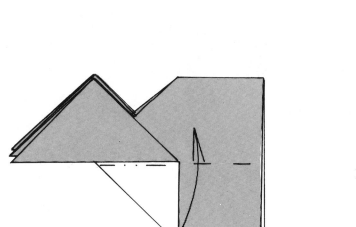

9. Reverse-fold; repeat behind.

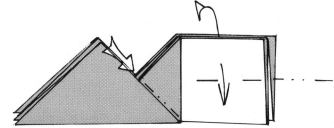

10. Reverse-fold; repeat behind.

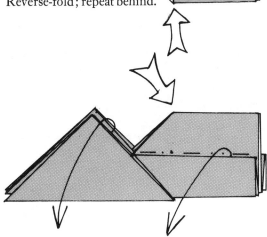

11. Sink flap while opening model.

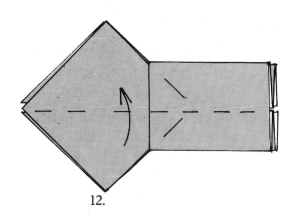

12.

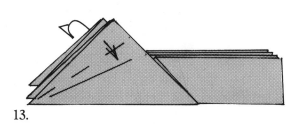

13.

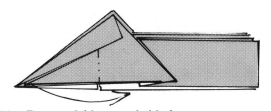

14. Reverse-fold; repeat behind.

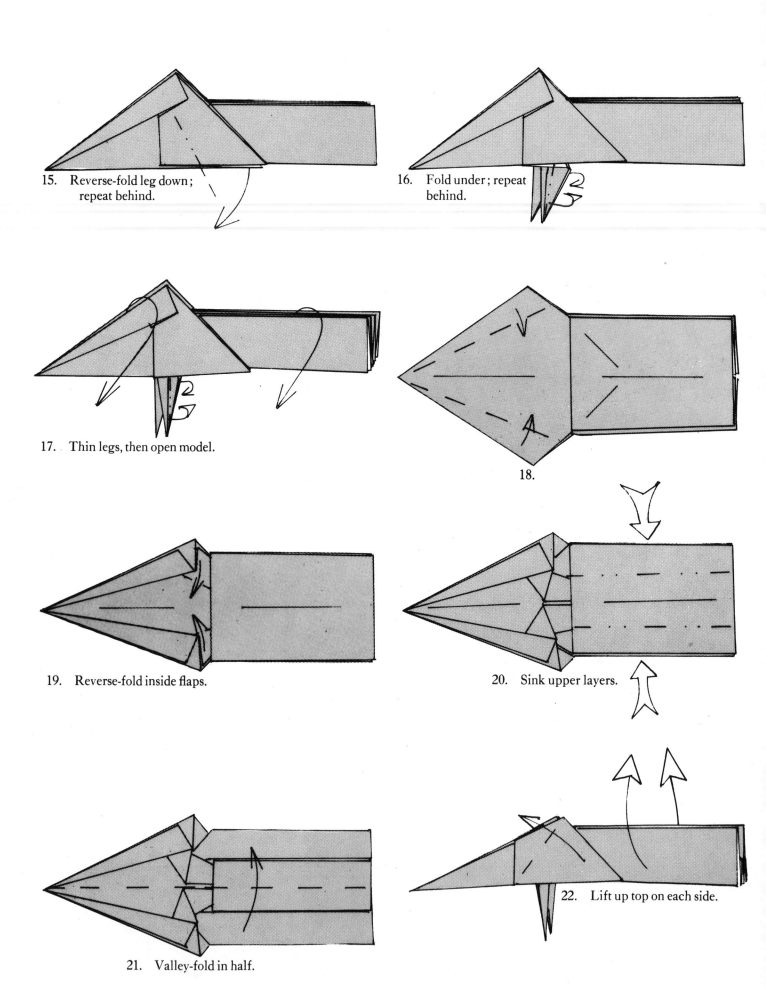

15. Reverse-fold leg down; repeat behind.

16. Fold under; repeat behind.

17. Thin legs, then open model.

18.

19. Reverse-fold inside flaps.

20. Sink upper layers.

21. Valley-fold in half.

22. Lift up top on each side.

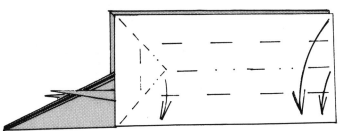

23.   Pleat-fold in quarters; repeat behind.

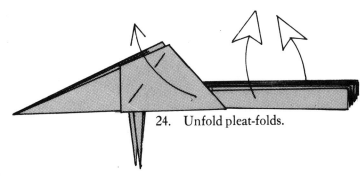

24.   Unfold pleat-folds.

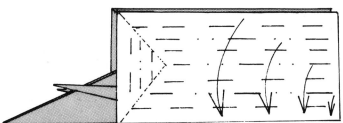

25.   Pleat-fold in eighths; repeat behind.

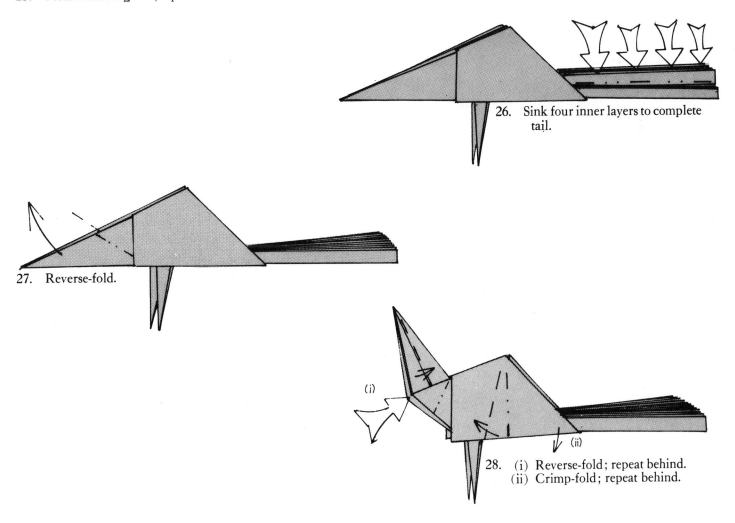

26.   Sink four inner layers to complete tail.

27.   Reverse-fold.

28.   (i) Reverse-fold; repeat behind.
       (ii) Crimp-fold; repeat behind.

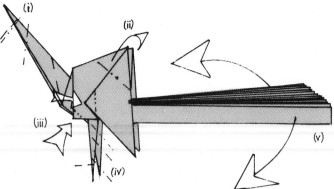

29. (i) Outside reverse-fold twice to form head and neck, then crimp-fold to form beak.
    (ii) Fold inside.
    (iii) Inside reverse-fold.
    (iv) Inside reverse-fold twice to form legs, then crimp-fold to form feet.
    (v) Spread tail.

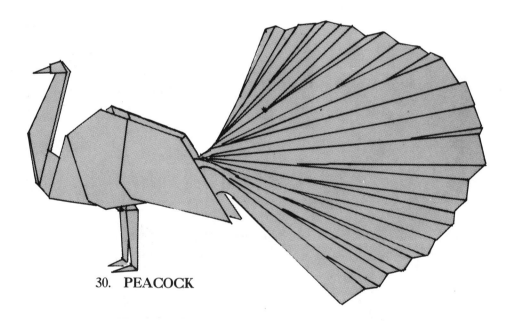

30. PEACOCK

RABBIT

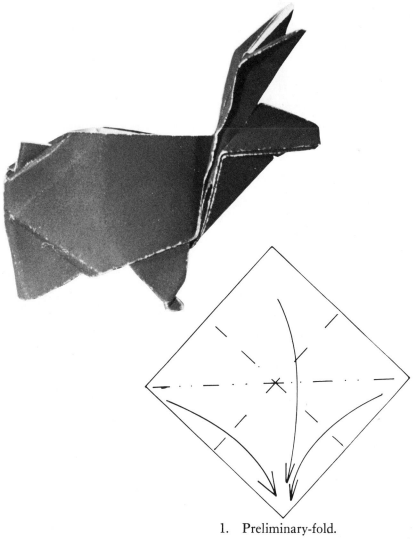

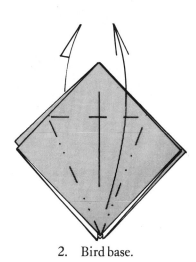

1. Preliminary-fold.

2. Bird base.

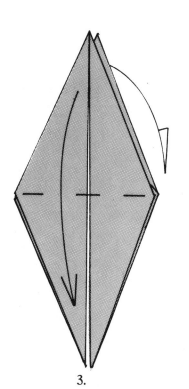

3.

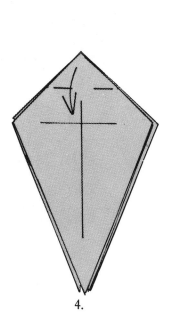

4.

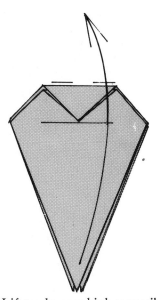

5. Lift top layer as high as possible.
   (Model will open slightly.)

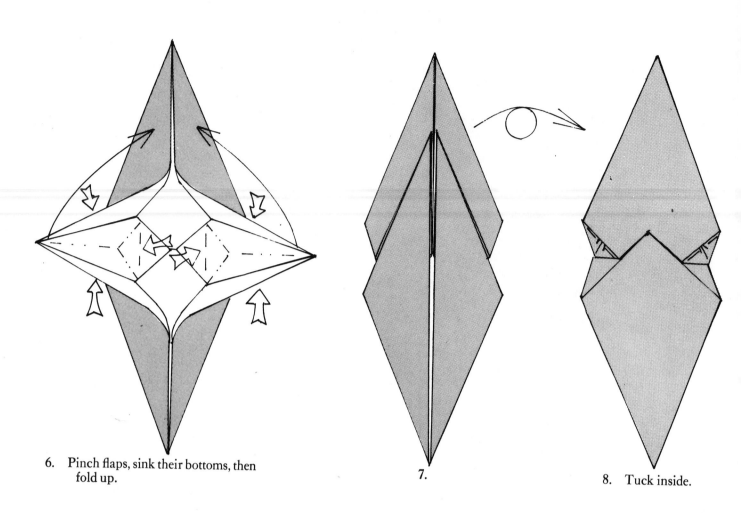

6. Pinch flaps, sink their bottoms, then
   fold up.

7.

8. Tuck inside.

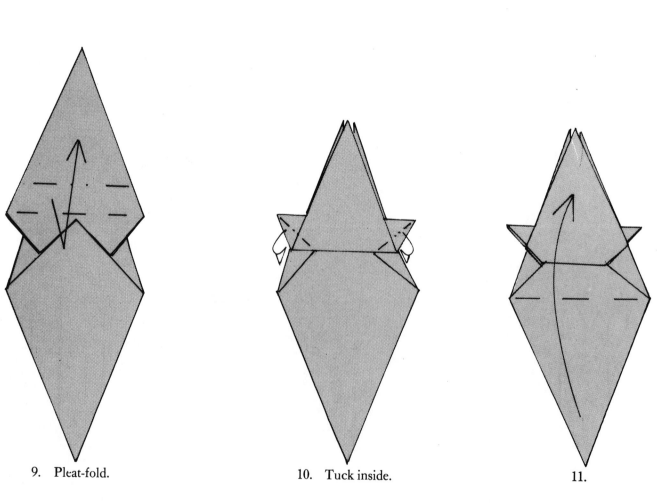

9. Pleat-fold.

10. Tuck inside.

11.

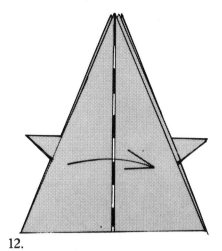

12.

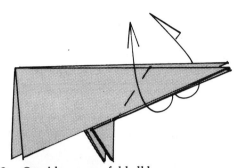

13. Outside reverse-fold all layers together.

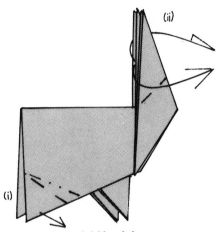

14. (i) Pleat-fold back layer.
    (ii) Outside reverse-fold two layers together.

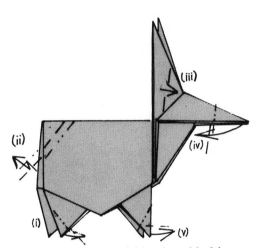

15. (i) Reverse-fold to form hind feet.
    (ii) Crimp-fold to form tail.
    (iii) Open ears.
    (iv) Reverse-fold nose.
    (v) Crimp-fold to form front feet.

16. **RABBIT**

SKUNK

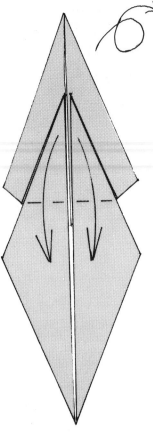

1. Begin by turning over step 8 of rabbit.

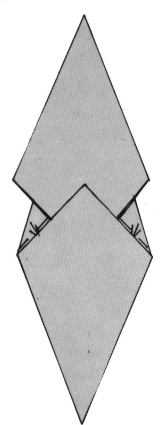

2. Tuck inside.

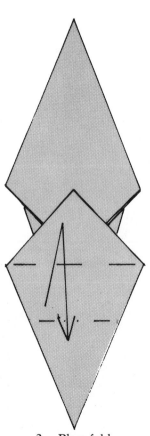

3. Pleat-fold.

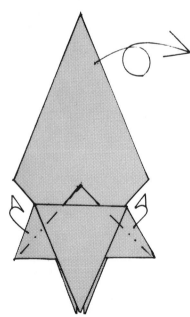

4. Tuck inside. Turn model over.

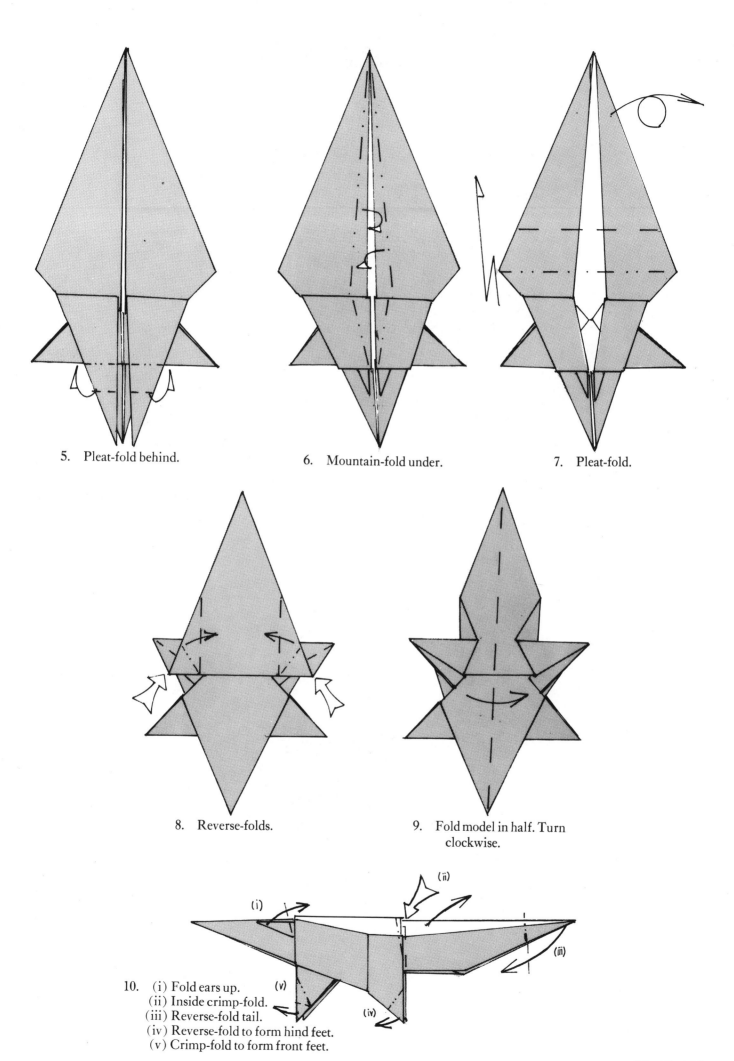

5. Pleat-fold behind.

6. Mountain-fold under.

7. Pleat-fold.

8. Reverse-folds.

9. Fold model in half. Turn clockwise.

(i)

(ii)

(iii)

(iv)

(v)

10. (i) Fold ears up.
(ii) Inside crimp-fold.
(iii) Reverse-fold tail.
(iv) Reverse-fold to form hind feet.
(v) Crimp-fold to form front feet.

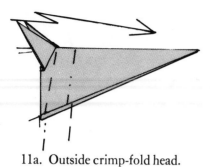

11a. Outside crimp-fold head.

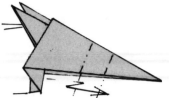

11b. Inside crimp-fold nose.

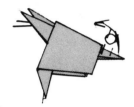

11c. Outside reverse-fold twice.

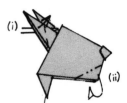

11d. (i) Reverse-fold ears.
(ii) Tuck inside; repeat behind.

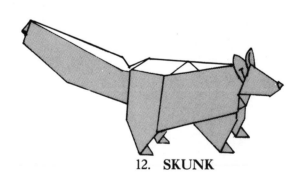

12. SKUNK

MOUSE

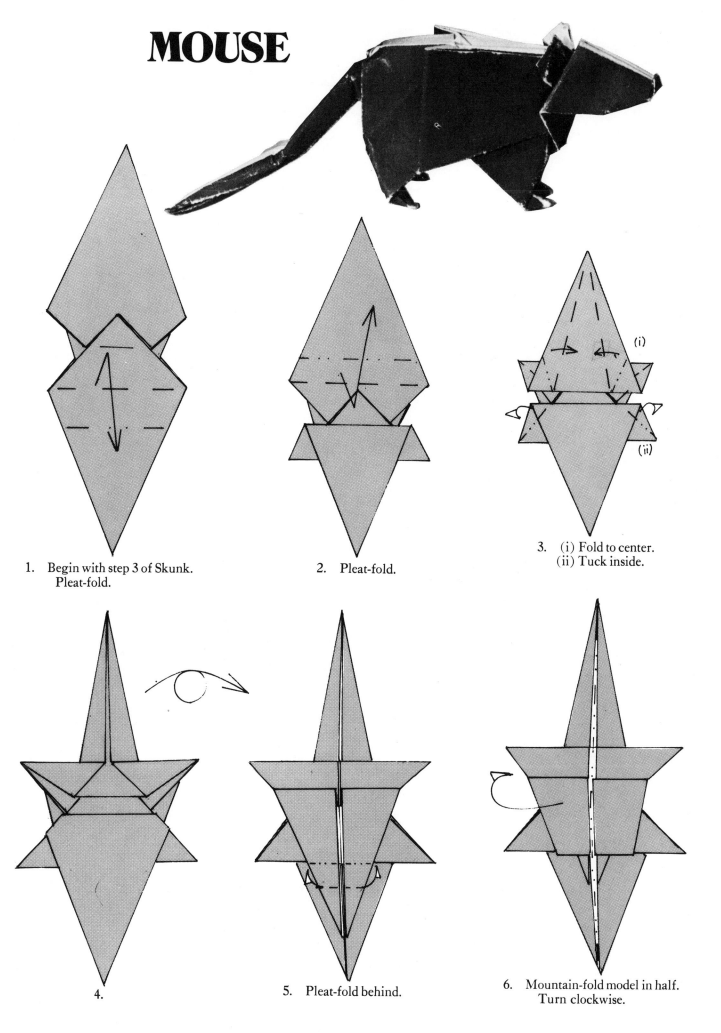

1. Begin with step 3 of Skunk. Pleat-fold.

2. Pleat-fold.

3. (i) Fold to center.
   (ii) Tuck inside.

4.

5. Pleat-fold behind.

6. Mountain-fold model in half. Turn clockwise.

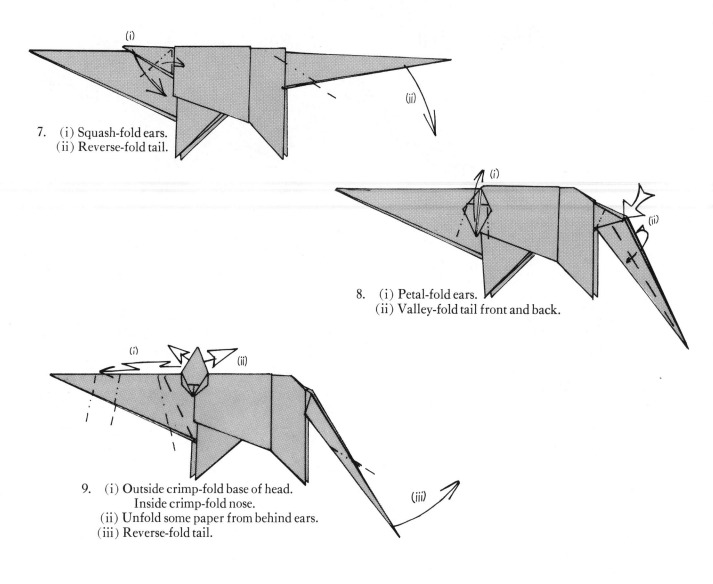

7. (i) Squash-fold ears.
   (ii) Reverse-fold tail.

8. (i) Petal-fold ears.
   (ii) Valley-fold tail front and back.

9. (i) Outside crimp-fold base of head.
       Inside crimp-fold nose.
   (ii) Unfold some paper from behind ears.
   (iii) Reverse-fold tail.

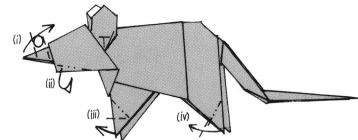

10. (i) Fold nose over twice.
    (ii) Fold inside; repeat behind.
    (iii) Crimp-fold to form front feet.
    (iv) Reverse-fold to form hind feet.

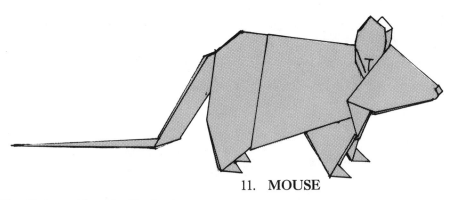

11. MOUSE

SQUIRREL

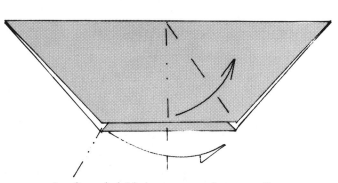

1. Kite-fold and unfold two opposite corners, then mountain-fold along guidelines.

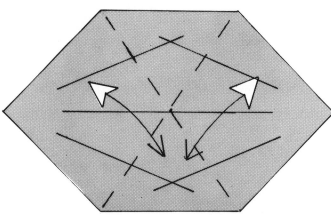

2. Fold and unfold along dashed lines.

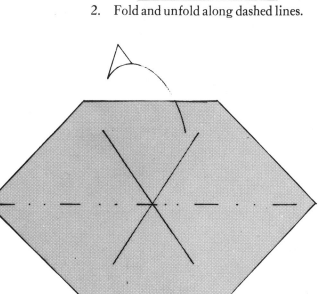

3. Mountain-fold model in half.

4. Squash-fold along creases from step 2.

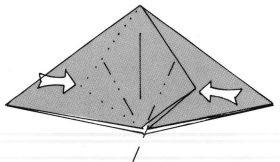

5. Reverse-fold; repeat behind.

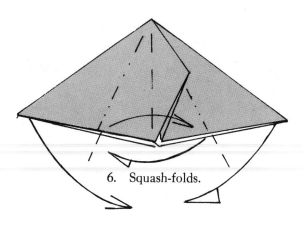

6. Squash-folds.

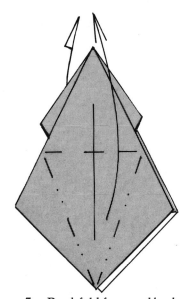

7. Petal-fold front and back.

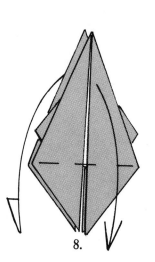

8.

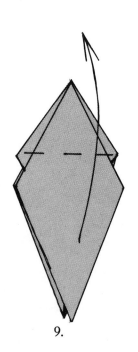

9.

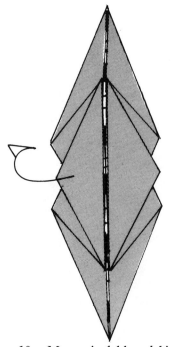

10. Mountain-fold model in half.
Turn counterclockwise.

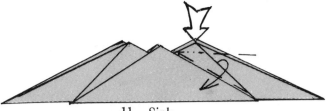

11. Sink.

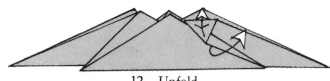

12. Unfold.

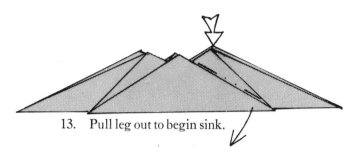

13. Pull leg out to begin sink.

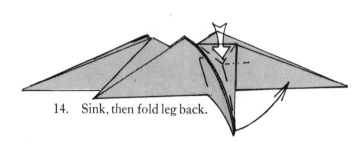

14. Sink, then fold leg back.

15. Repeat steps 11–14 on three remaining sides.

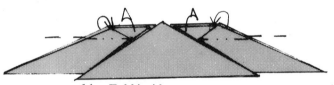

16. Fold inside.

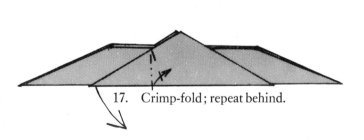

17. Crimp-fold; repeat behind.

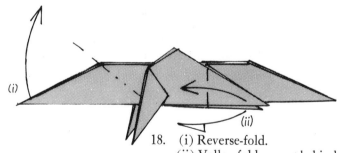

18. (i) Reverse-fold.
    (ii) Valley-fold; repeat behind.

19. Outside crimp-fold. (Head section will separate from body slightly.)

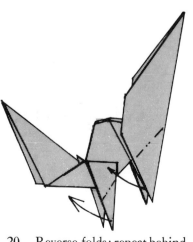

20. Reverse-folds; repeat behind.

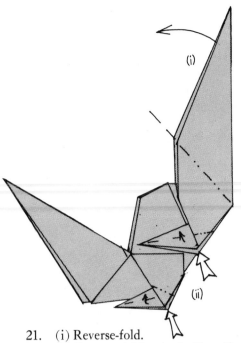

21. (i) Reverse-fold.
    (ii) Reverse-fold on both sides of leg;
        repeat behind.

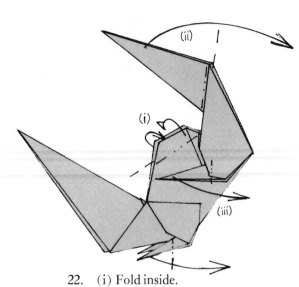

22. (i) Fold inside.
    (ii) Reverse-fold.
    (iii) Reverse-fold legs; repeat behind.

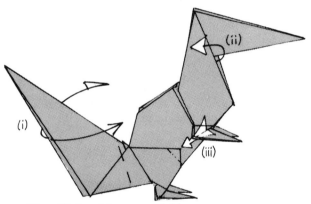

23. (i) Outside reverse-fold.
    (ii) Pull out layer from inside of neck
        and fold to left; repeat behind.
    (iii) Reverse-fold; repeat behind.

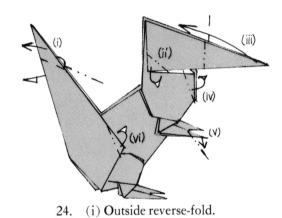

24. (i) Outside reverse-fold.
    (ii) Mountain-fold.
    (iii) Inside reverse-fold.
    (iv) Mountain-fold.
    (v) Inside reverse-fold.
    (vi) Mountain-fold.

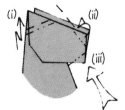

25. (i) Pleat-fold ears.
    (ii) Mountain-fold.
    (iii) Reverse-fold.

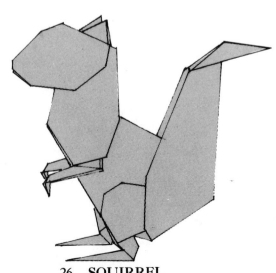

26. **SQUIRREL**

RHINOCEROS

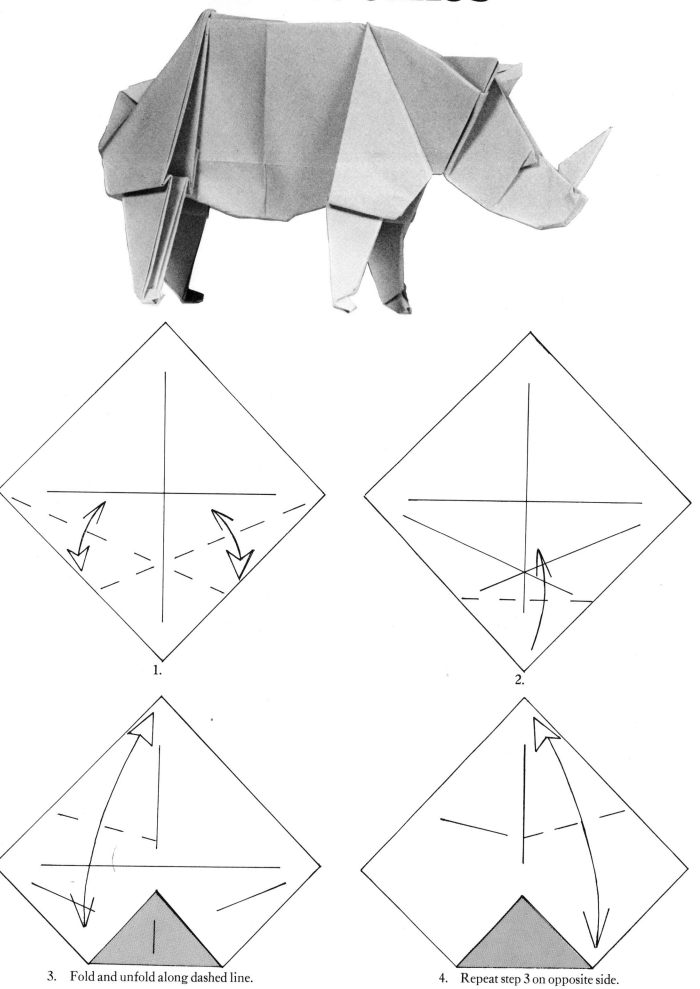

1.

2.

3. Fold and unfold along dashed line.

4. Repeat step 3 on opposite side.

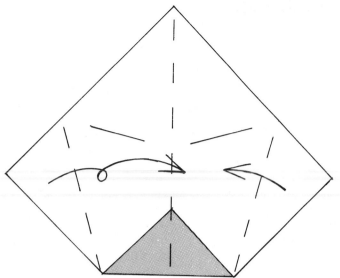

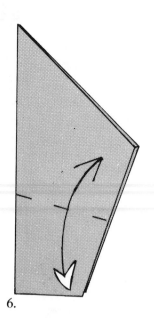

5. Fold flaps as shown, then fold model in half.

6.

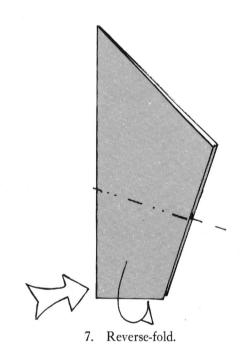

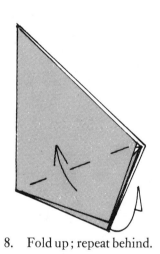

7. Reverse-fold.

8. Fold up; repeat behind.

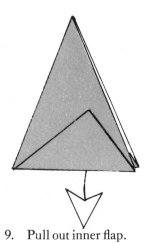

9. Pull out inner flap.

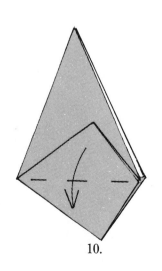

10.

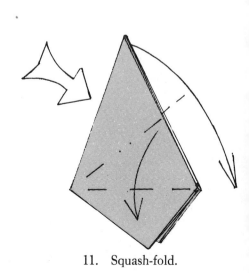

11. Squash-fold.

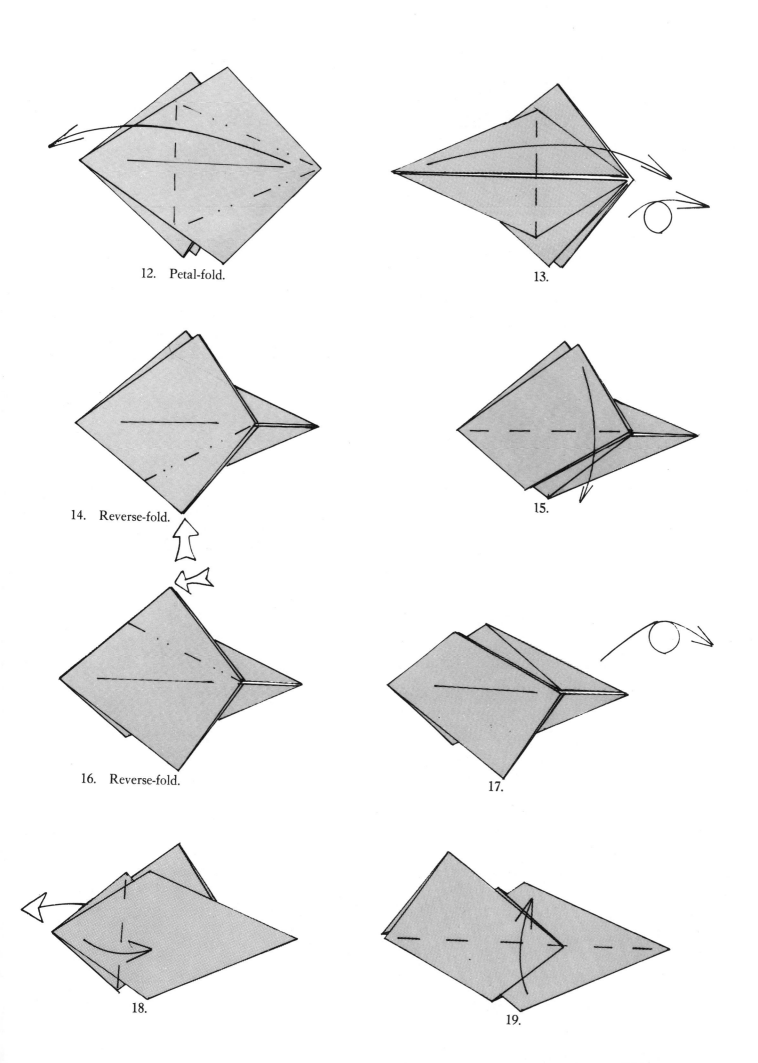

12.   Petal-fold.

13.

14.   Reverse-fold.

15.

16.   Reverse-fold.

17.

18.

19.

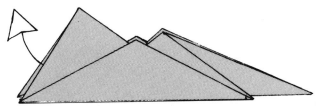

20. Pull out inner layer.

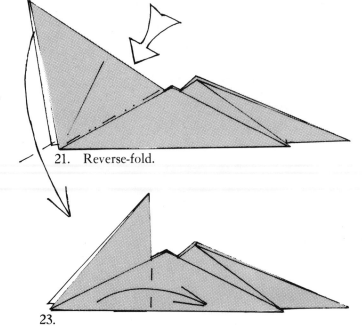

21. Reverse-fold.

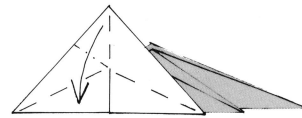

22. Reverse-fold.

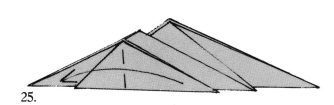

23.

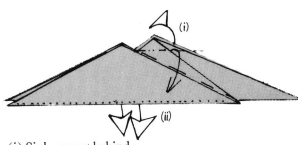

24. Rabbit ear.

25.

26. (i) Sink; repeat behind.
    (ii) Pull out all inside layers connected to side marked by dotted line; repeat behind.

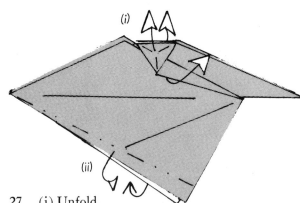

27. (i) Unfold.
    (ii) Fold inside; repeat behind.

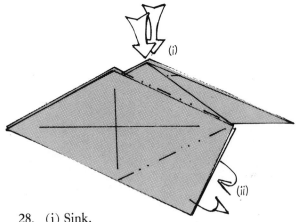

28. (i) Sink.
    (ii) Fold inside.

29. (i) Valley-fold.
    (ii) Rabbit ear; repeat behind.

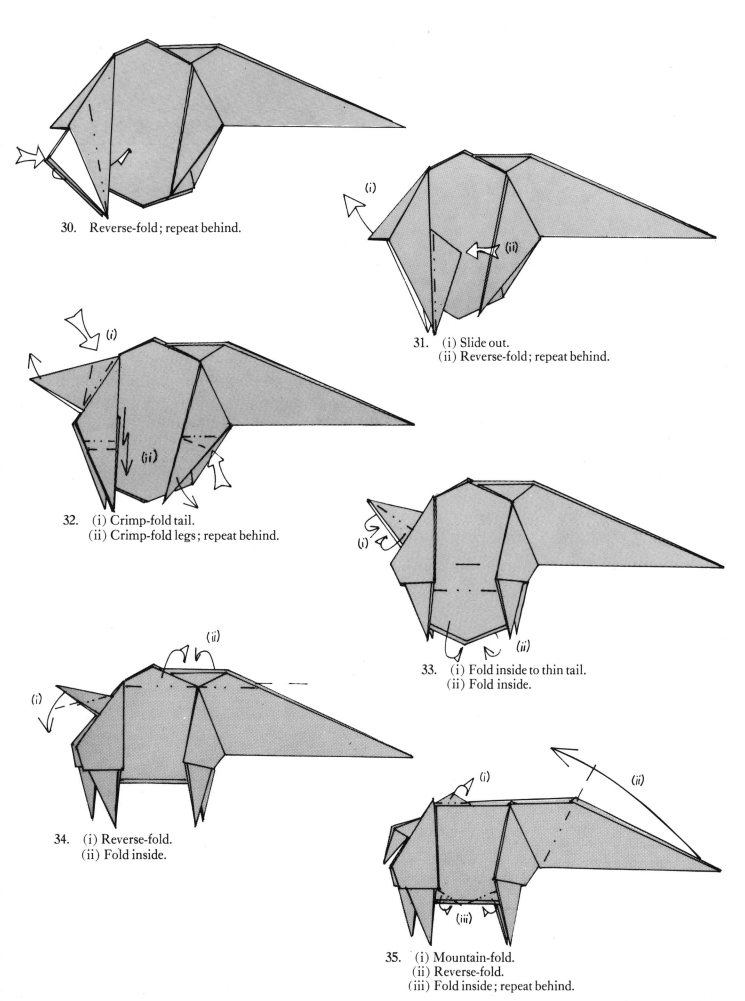

30. Reverse-fold; repeat behind.

31. (i) Slide out.
    (ii) Reverse-fold; repeat behind.

32. (i) Crimp-fold tail.
    (ii) Crimp-fold legs; repeat behind.

33. (i) Fold inside to thin tail.
    (ii) Fold inside.

34. (i) Reverse-fold.
    (ii) Fold inside.

35. (i) Mountain-fold.
    (ii) Reverse-fold.
    (iii) Fold inside; repeat behind.

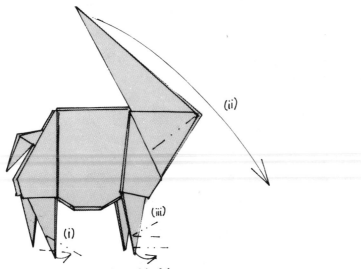

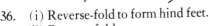

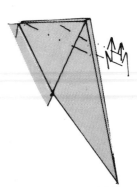

36. (i) Reverse-fold to form hind feet.
     (ii) Reverse-fold.
     (iii) Crimp-fold to form front feet.

37a. Pleat-fold.

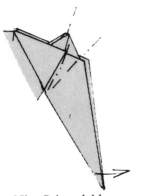

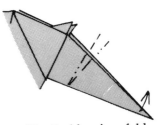

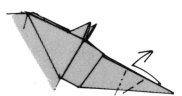

37d. Inside reverse-fold twice.

37c. Inside crimp-fold.

37b. Crimp-fold.

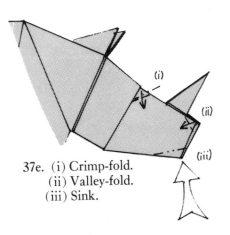

37e. (i) Crimp-fold.
      (ii) Valley-fold.
      (iii) Sink.

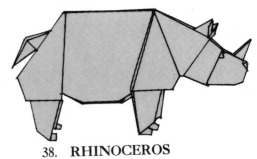

38. **RHINOCEROS**

ELEPHANT

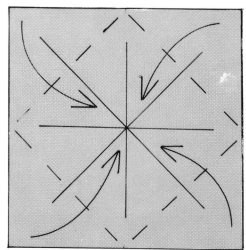

1. Blintz-fold.

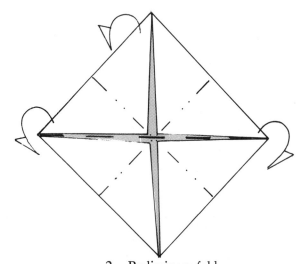

2. Preliminary-fold.

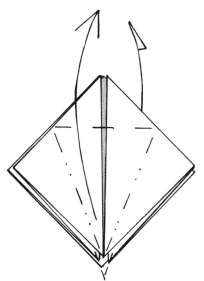

3. Petal-fold.

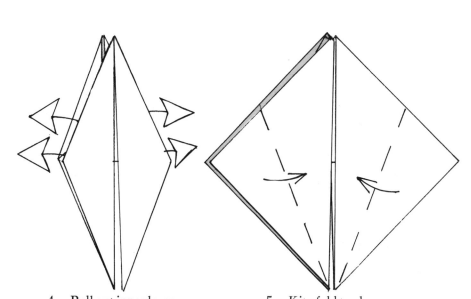

4. Pull out inner layers.

5. Kite-fold top layer.

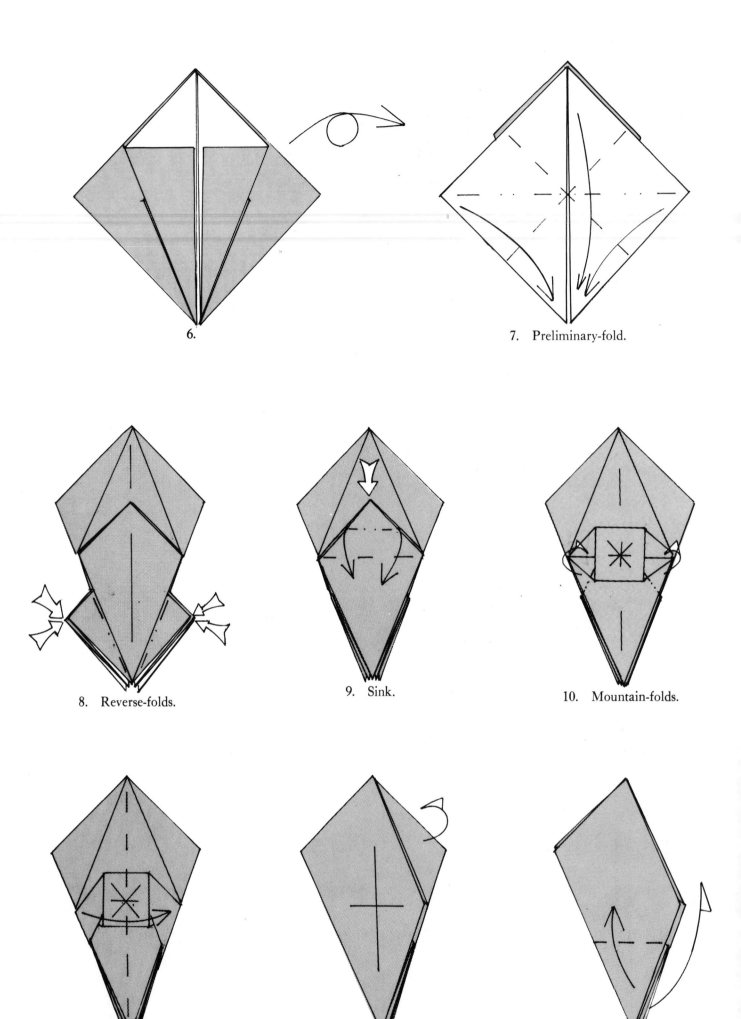

6.

7. Preliminary-fold.

8. Reverse-folds.

9. Sink.

10. Mountain-folds.

11.

12.

13.

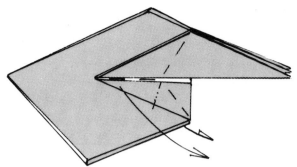

14. Rabbit ear; repeat behind.

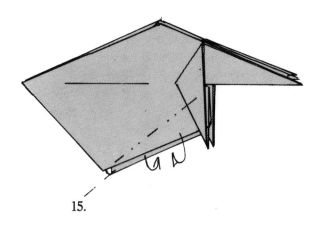

15.

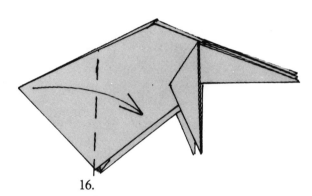

16.

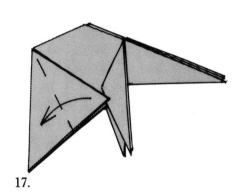

17.

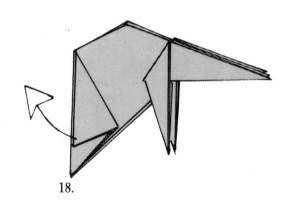

18.

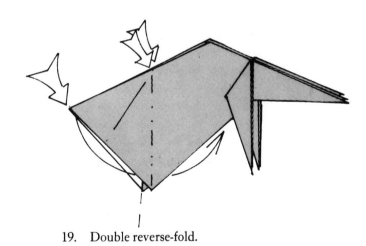

19. Double reverse-fold.

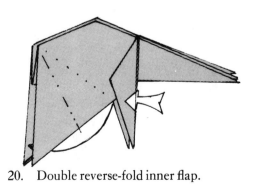

20. Double reverse-fold inner flap.

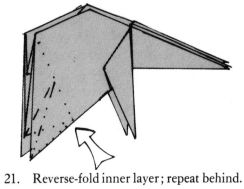

21. Reverse-fold inner layer; repeat behind.

Elephant 69

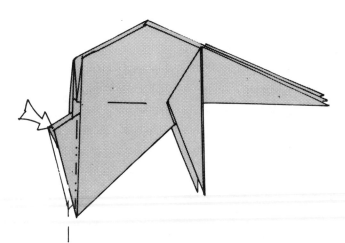

22. Reverse-fold; repeat behind.

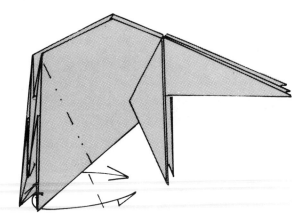

23. Reverse-fold; repeat behind. (Fold is not symmetrical.)

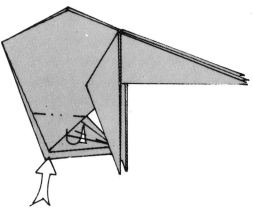

24. Reverse-fold; repeat behind.

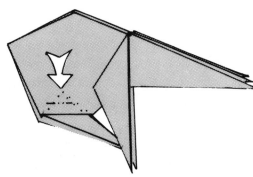

25. Reverse-fold inside layer; repeat behind.

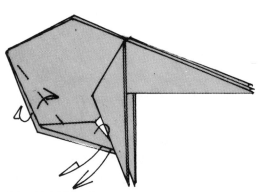

26. Fold legs down.

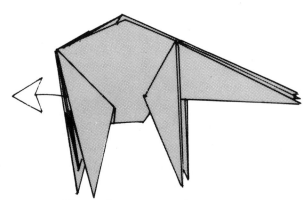

27. Pull out trapped flap.

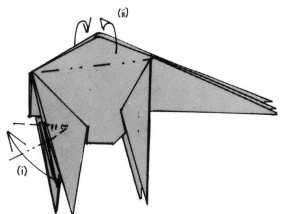

28. (i) Crimp-fold to form tail.
    (ii) Fold inside.

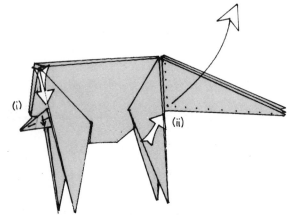

29. (i) Reverse-fold; repeat behind.
    (ii) Pull out the two layers between the three flaps.

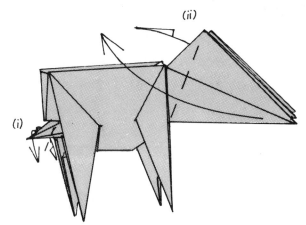

30. (i) Outside reverse-fold tail.
    (ii) Valley-fold outer layer; repeat behind.

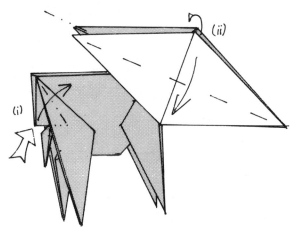

31. (i) Reverse-fold.
    (ii) Valley-fold; repeat behind.

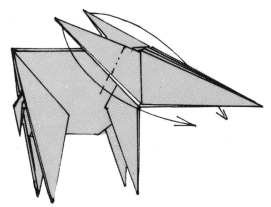

32. Reverse-fold; repeat behind.

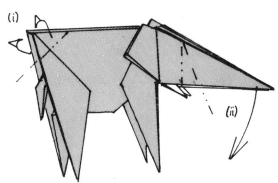

33. (i) Fold inside.
    (ii) Inside crimp-fold trunk. (Fold is not symmetrical.)

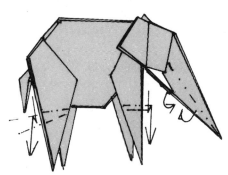

34. Crimp-fold legs; repeat behind.

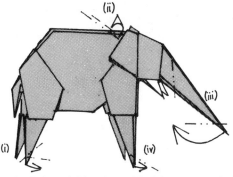

35. (i) Crimp-fold to form hind feet; repeat behind.
    (ii) Fold inside; repeat behind.
    (iii) Reverse-fold twice.
    (iv) Reverse-fold to form front feet; repeat behind.

36. ELEPHANT

MOUNTAIN GOAT

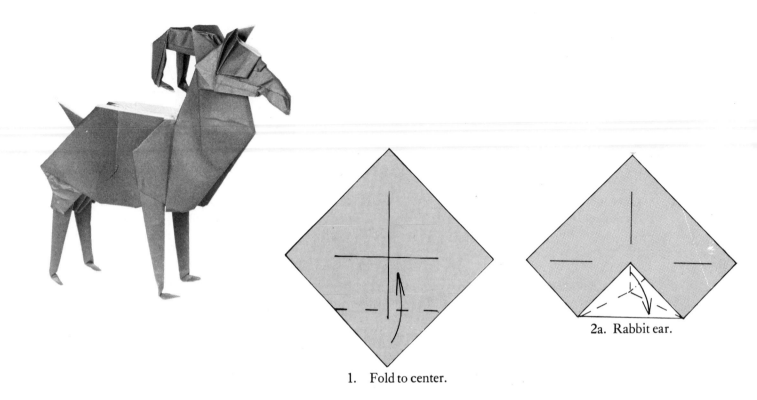

1. Fold to center.

2a. Rabbit ear.

2b. Squash-fold.

2c. Petal-fold.

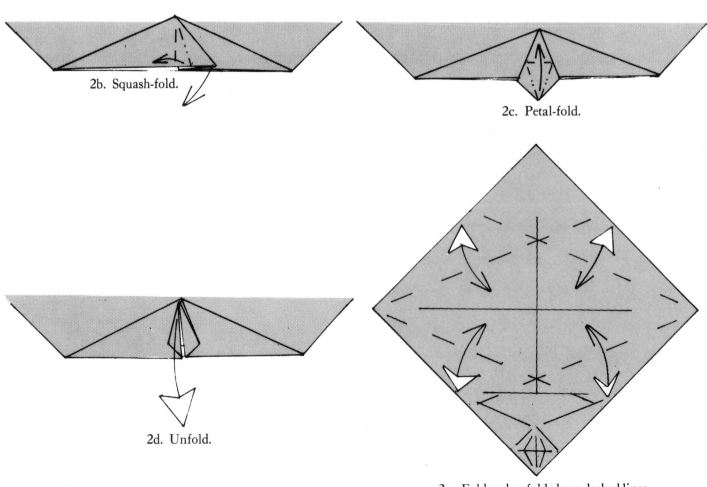

2d. Unfold.

3. Fold and unfold along dashed lines.

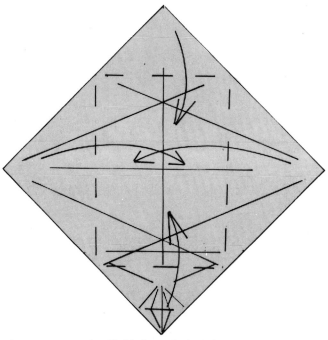

4. Fold along dashed lines.

5. Mountain-fold model in half.

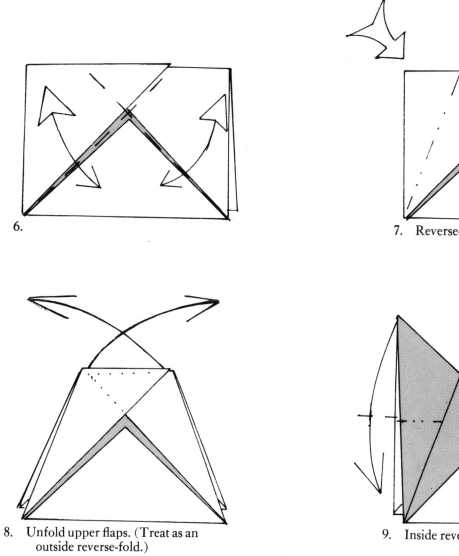

6.

7. Reverse-folds.

8. Unfold upper flaps. (Treat as an outside reverse-fold.)

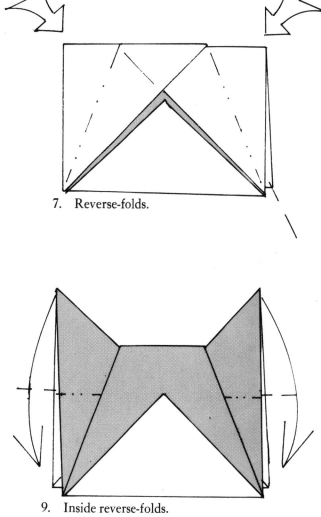

9. Inside reverse-folds.

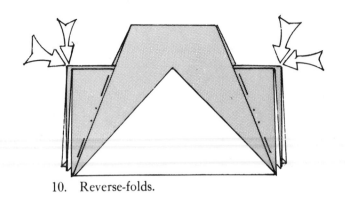

10. Reverse-folds.

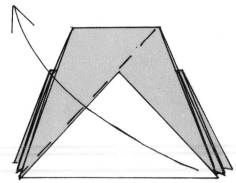

11. Fold up as in stretched bird base.

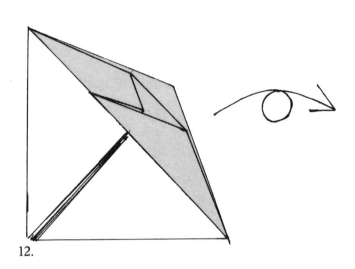

12.

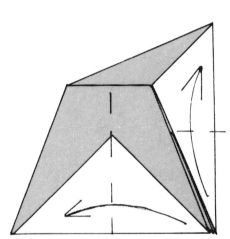

13. Fold up as in stretched bird base.

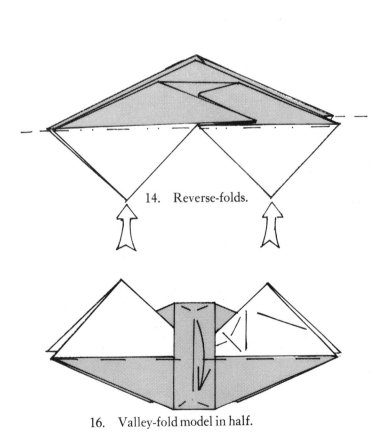

14. Reverse-folds.

16. Valley-fold model in half.

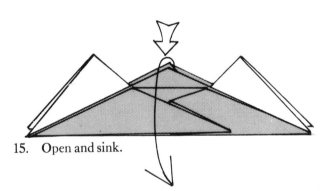

15. Open and sink.

17. (i) Reverse-fold.
     (ii) Reverse-fold and snap top layer up.

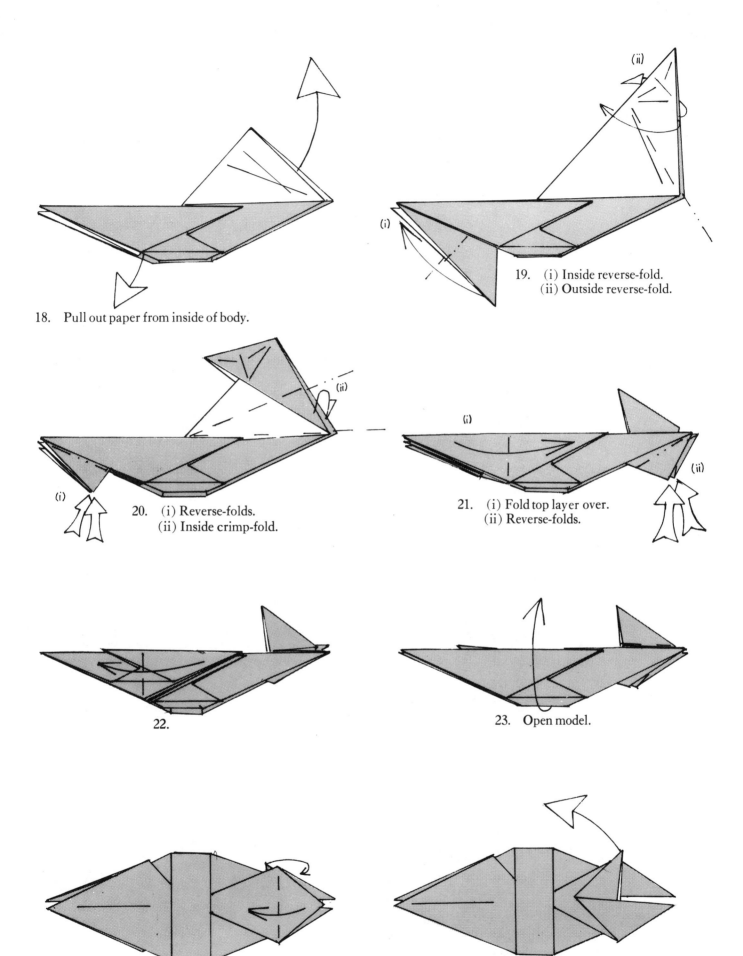

18. Pull out paper from inside of body.

19. (i) Inside reverse-fold.
     (ii) Outside reverse-fold.

20. (i) Reverse-folds.
     (ii) Inside crimp-fold.

21. (i) Fold top layer over.
     (ii) Reverse-folds.

22.

23. Open model.

24.

25. Fold flap out.

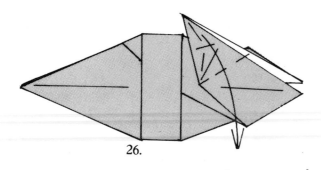

26.

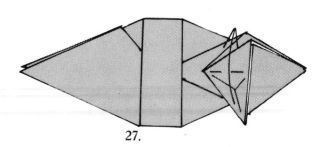

27.

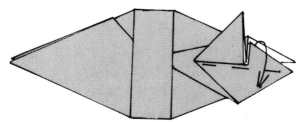

28.   Valley-fold inner layer.

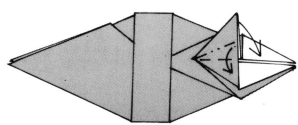

29.   Squash-fold.

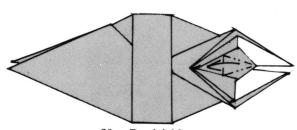

30.   Petal-fold.

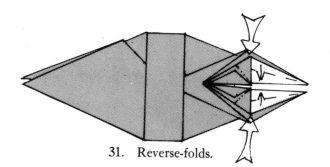

31.   Reverse-folds.

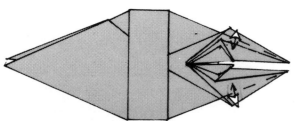

32.   Fold and unfold as shown.

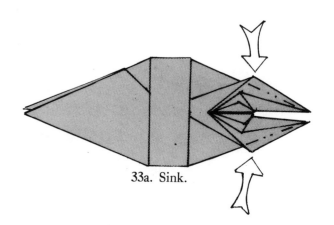

33a. Sink.

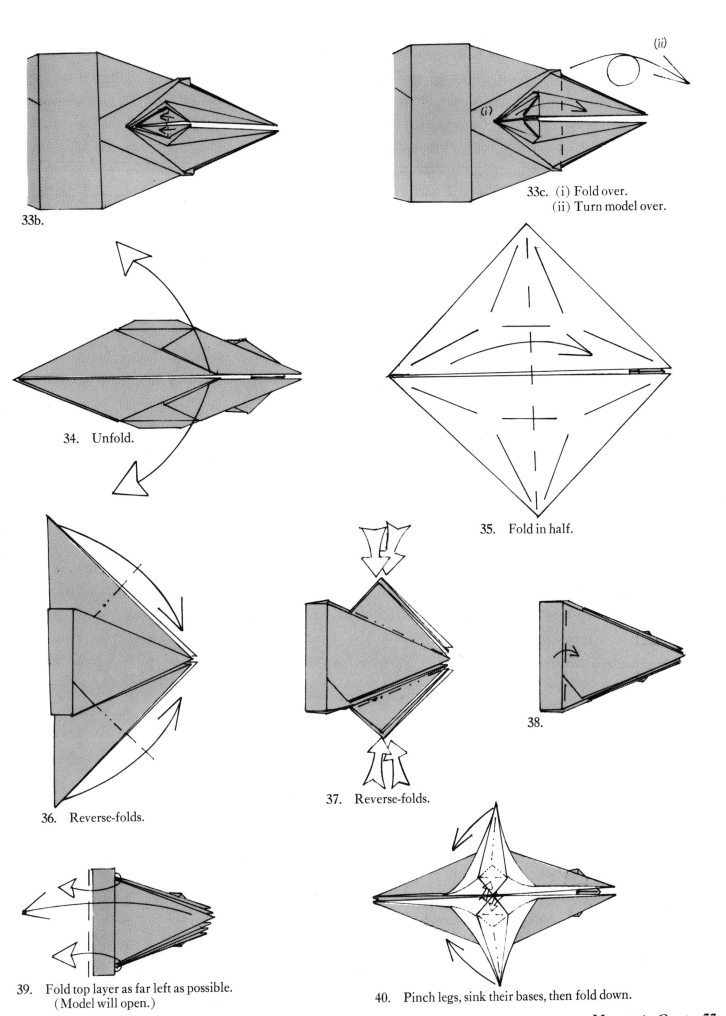

33b.

33c. (i) Fold over.
(ii) Turn model over.

34. Unfold.

35. Fold in half.

36. Reverse-folds.

37. Reverse-folds.

38.

39. Fold top layer as far left as possible.
(Model will open.)

40. Pinch legs, sink their bases, then fold down.

Mountain Goat 77

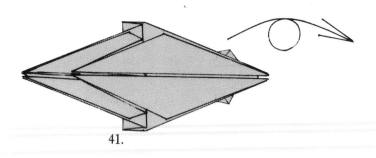

41.

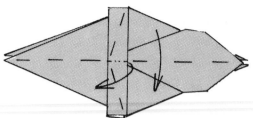

42. Reverse-fold middle flap while folding model in half.

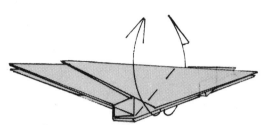

43. Outside reverse-fold.

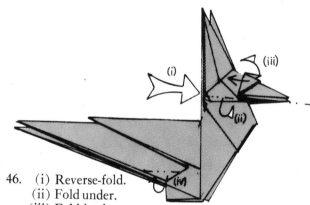

44. Valley-fold inside flap on layer above.

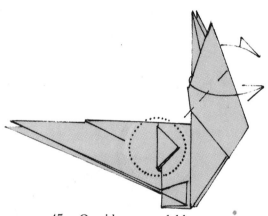

45. Outside reverse-fold.

46. (i) Reverse-fold.
    (ii) Fold under.
    (iii) Fold back.
    (iv) Fold under. Repeat steps (i)–(iv) behind.

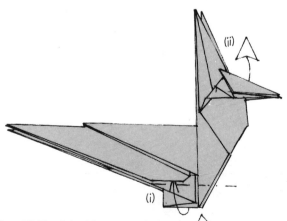

47. (i) Tuck inside; repeat behind.
    (ii) Lift up two layers from behind head.

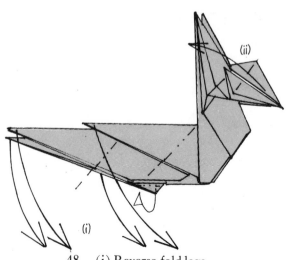

48. (i) Reverse-fold legs.
    (ii) Fold flap up.

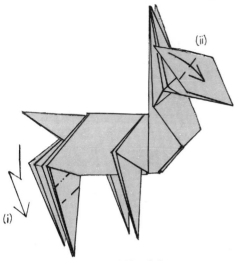

49. (i) Crimp-fold back legs.
    (ii) Fold flap down.

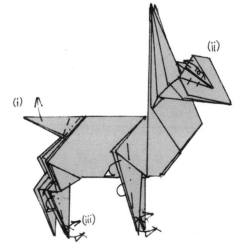

50a. (i) Crimp-fold tail.
     (ii) Fold over as shown.
     (iii) Fold some paper inside on each leg
          and crimp-fold to form feet.

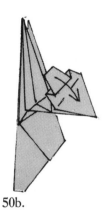

50b.

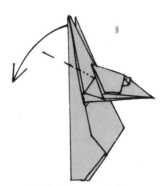

50c. (i) Fold inside.
     (ii) Fold head in
         half.

50d. Reverse-fold; repeat
     behind.

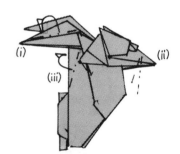

50e. (i) Fold inside; repeat
         behind.
     (ii) Outside crimp-fold
         nose.
     (iii) Fold inside; repeat
         behind.

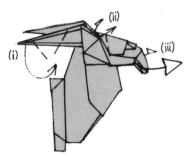

50f. (i) Reverse-fold horns twice.
     (ii) Fold out ears.
     (iii) Fold out nose.

51. **MOUNTAIN GOAT**

CAMEL

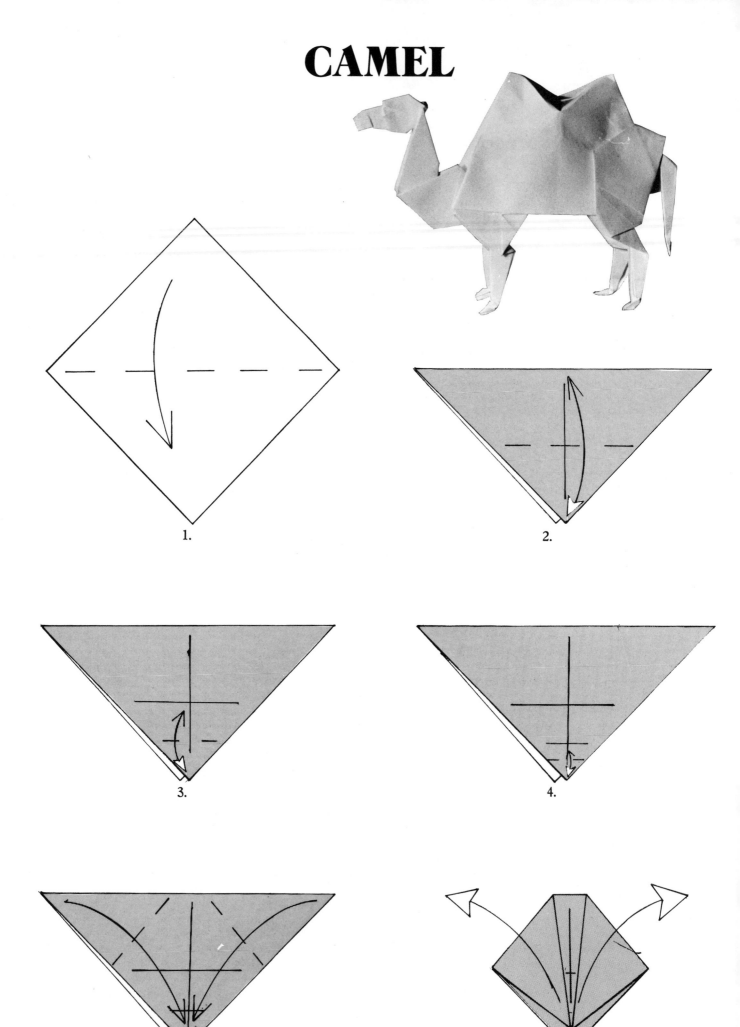

1.

2.

3.

4.

5.

6.

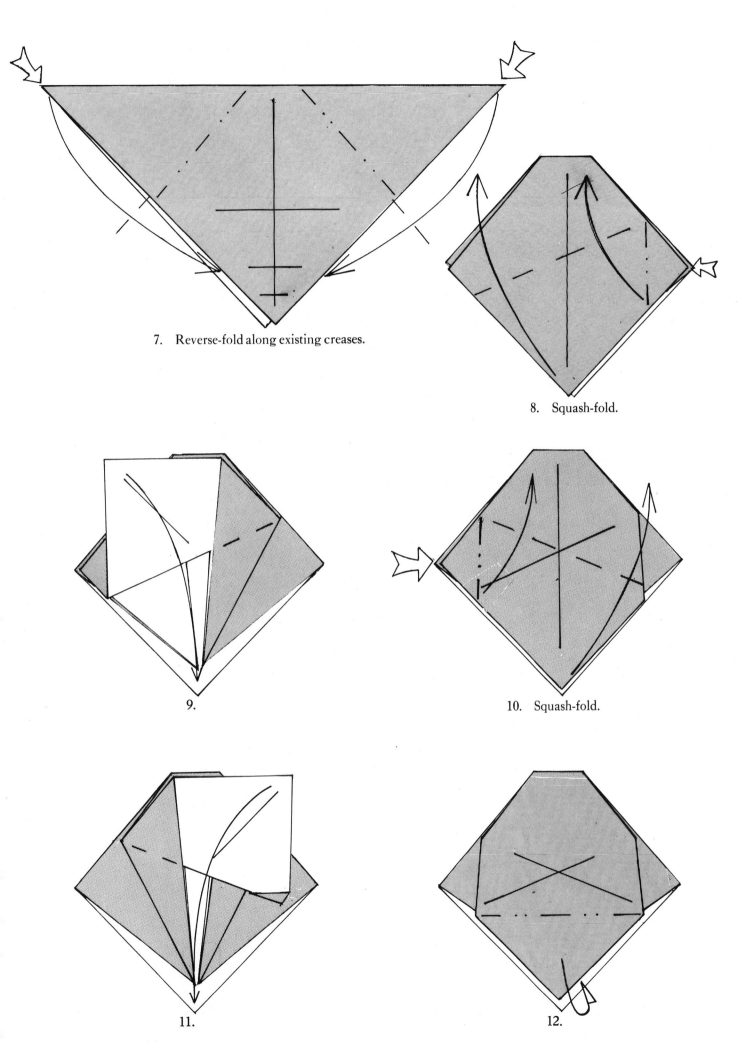

7. Reverse-fold along existing creases.

8. Squash-fold.

9.

10. Squash-fold.

11.

12.

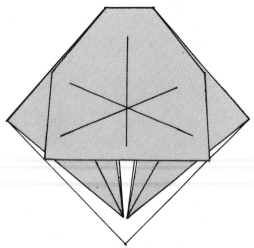

13.　Repeat steps 8–12 behind.

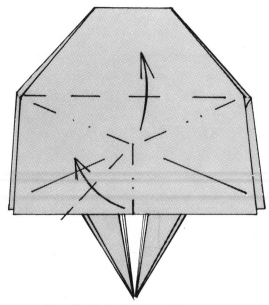

14.　Fold similar to rabbit ear.

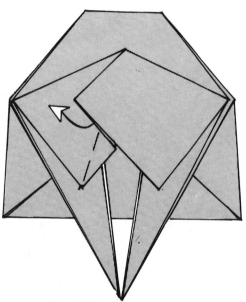

15.　Slide up.

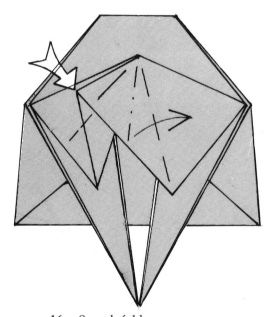

16.　Squash-fold.

17.　Petal-fold.

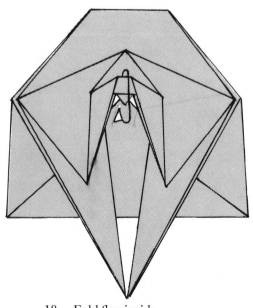

18.　Fold flap inside.

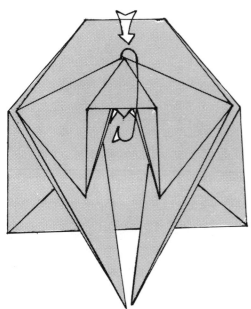

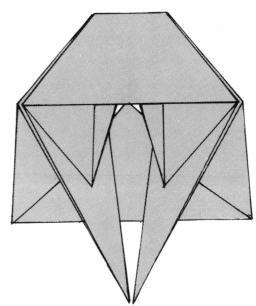

19.   Fold larger flap inside.

20.   Repeat steps 14–19 behind.

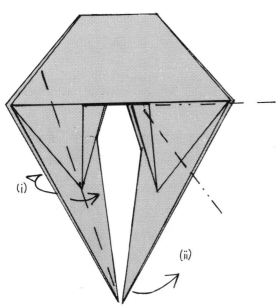

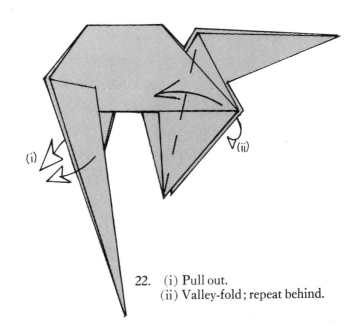

21.   (i) Valley-fold; repeat behind.
      (ii) Crimp-fold.

22.   (i) Pull out.
      (ii) Valley-fold; repeat behind.

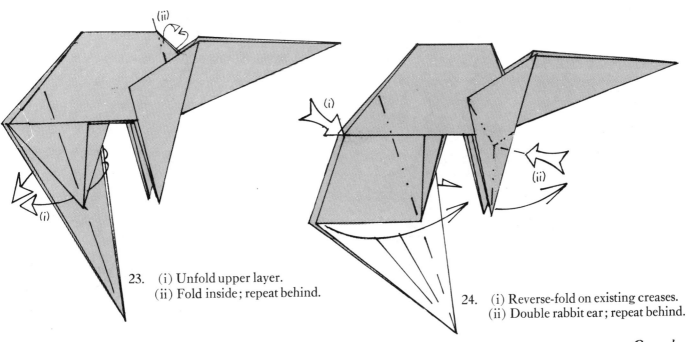

23.   (i) Unfold upper layer.
      (ii) Fold inside; repeat behind.

24.   (i) Reverse-fold on existing creases.
      (ii) Double rabbit ear; repeat behind.

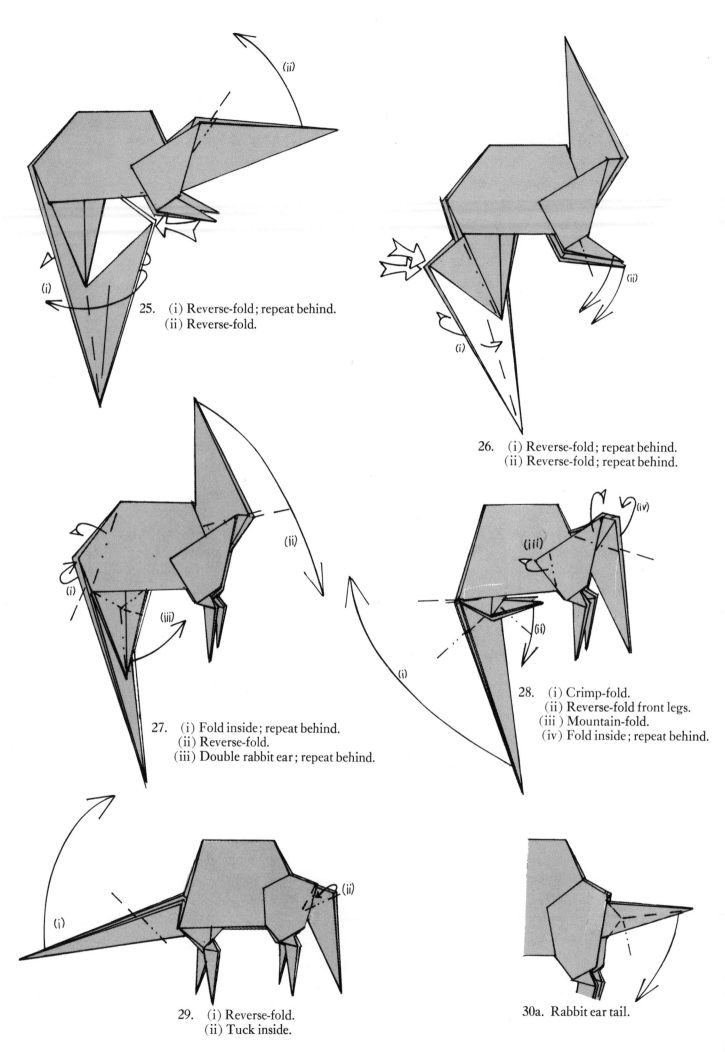

25. (i) Reverse-fold; repeat behind.
      (ii) Reverse-fold.

26. (i) Reverse-fold; repeat behind.
      (ii) Reverse-fold; repeat behind.

27. (i) Fold inside; repeat behind.
      (ii) Reverse-fold.
      (iii) Double rabbit ear; repeat behind.

28. (i) Crimp-fold.
      (ii) Reverse-fold front legs.
      (iii) Mountain-fold.
      (iv) Fold inside; repeat behind.

29. (i) Reverse-fold.
      (ii) Tuck inside.

30a. Rabbit ear tail.

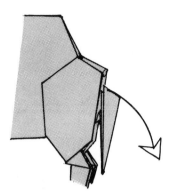

30b. Pull tail out.

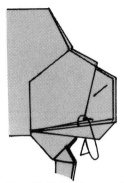

30c. Fold top layer to back.

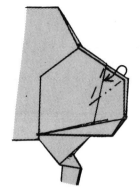

30d. Tuck back inside body.

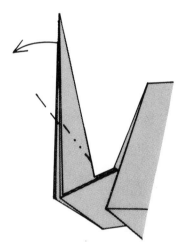

31a. Reverse-fold.

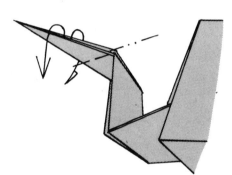

31b. Outside reverse-fold.

31c. Pull out one layer;
repeat behind.

31d. Inside crimp-fold.

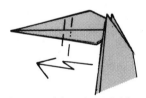

31e. Inside crimp-fold.

31f. Reverse-fold; repeat
behind.

31g. Pull up some of
top layer.

31h. Reverse-fold.

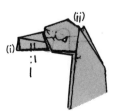

31i. (i) Outside crimp-fold nose.
(ii) Mountain-fold; repeat
behind.

Camel 85

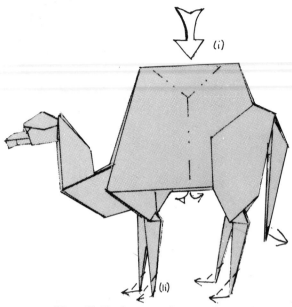

32. (i) Push center down and spread
 body apart.
 (ii) Outside reverse-fold to form feet;
 repeat behind.

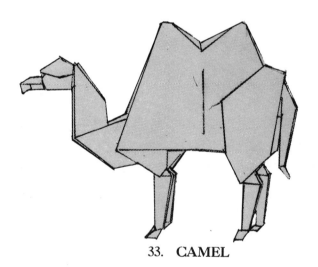

33. **CAMEL**

PEGASUS

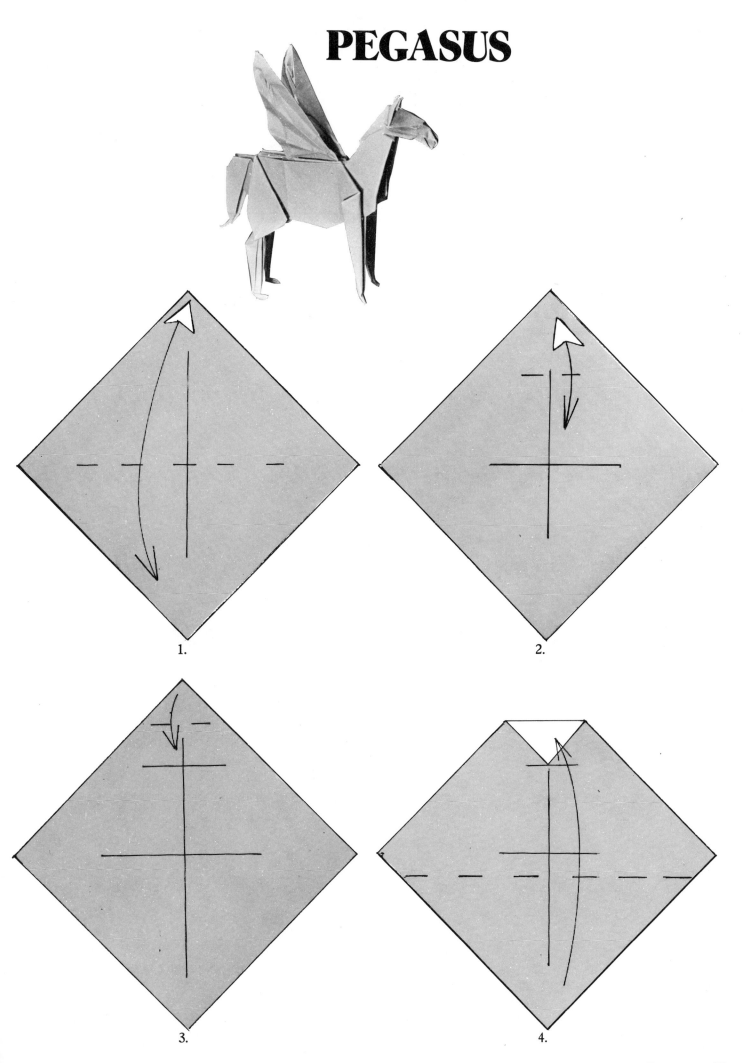

1.

2.

3.

4.

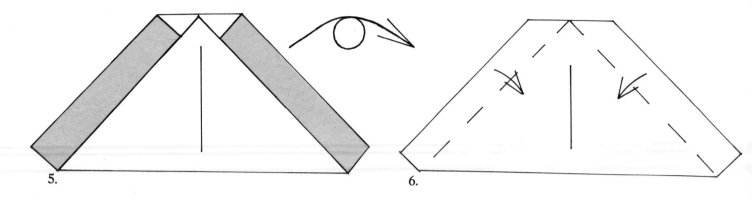

5.

6.

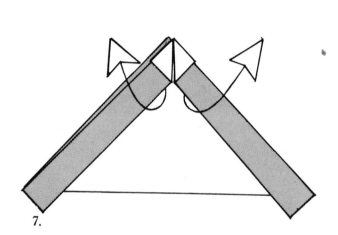

7.

8.   Unfold triangle from behind.

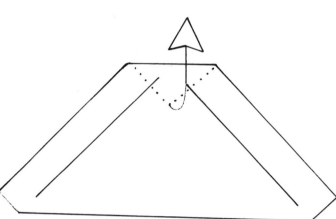

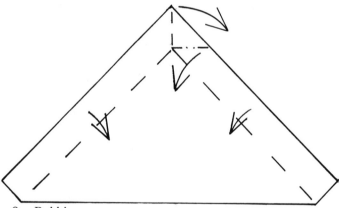

9.   Rabbit ear.

10a.   Squash-fold. (See details b, c, d.)

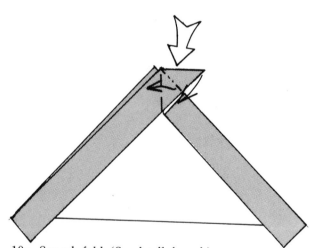

10b.   Squash-fold.

10c.   Petal-fold.

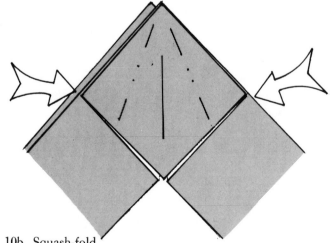

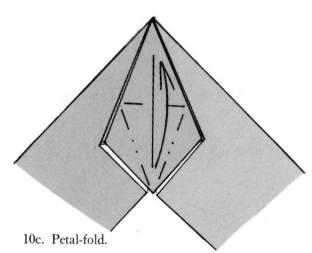

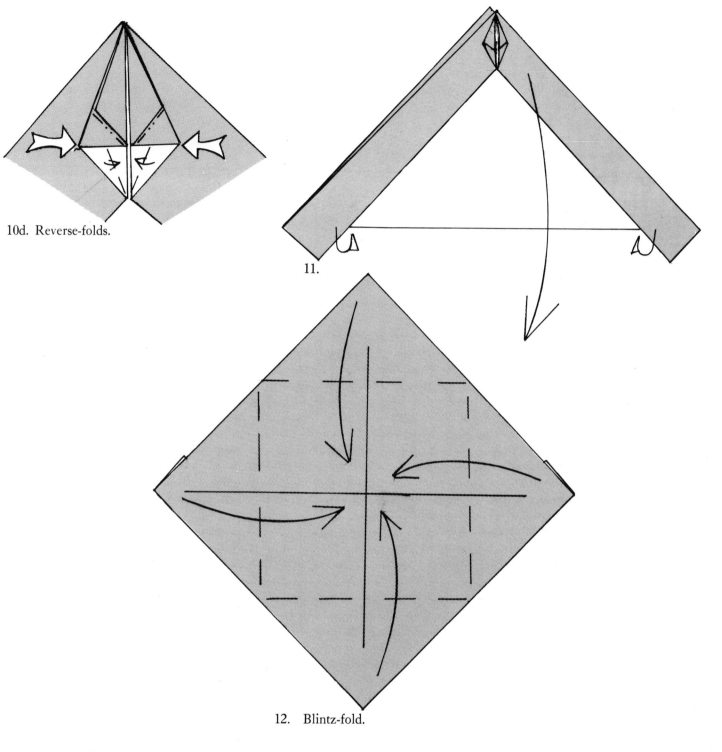

10d. Reverse-folds.

11.

12. Blintz-fold.

13. Preliminary-fold.

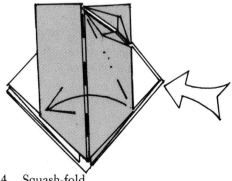

14. Squash-fold.

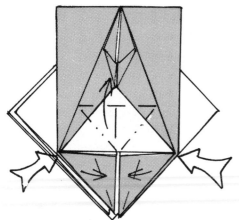

15. Petal-fold.

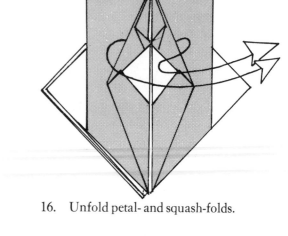

16. Unfold petal- and squash-folds.

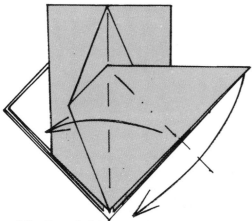

17. Squash-fold.

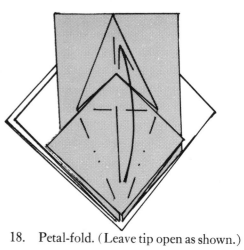

18. Petal-fold. (Leave tip open as shown.)

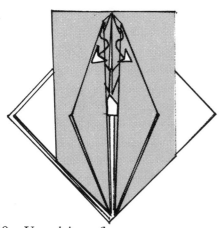

19. Untuck inner flaps.

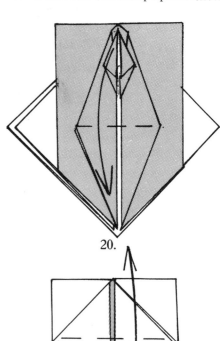

20.

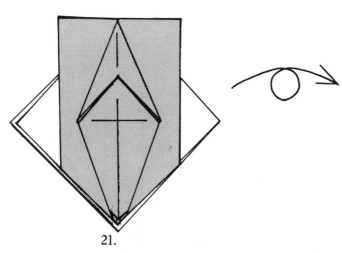

21.

22. Petal-fold.

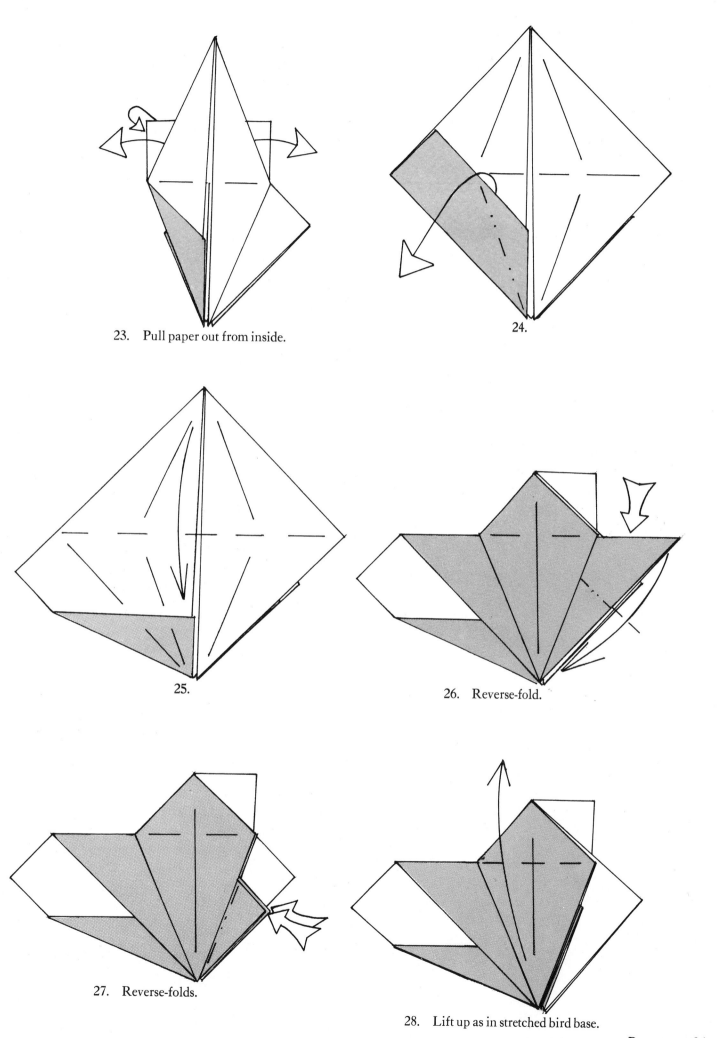

23. Pull paper out from inside.

24.

25.

26. Reverse-fold.

27. Reverse-folds.

28. Lift up as in stretched bird base.

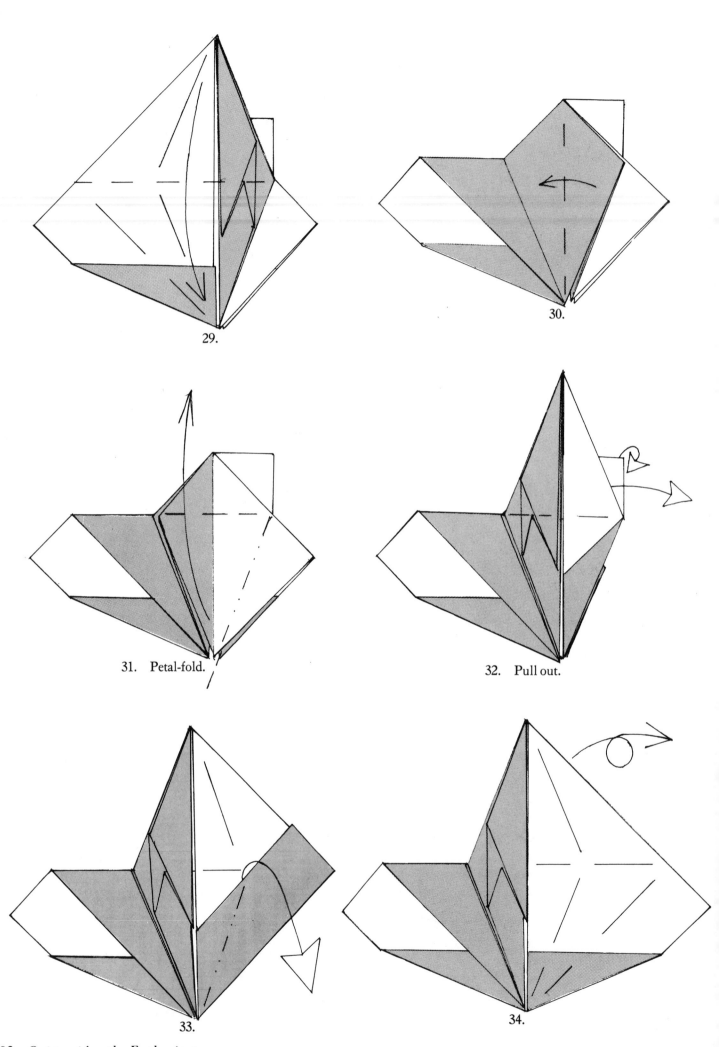

29.

30.

31. Petal-fold.

32. Pull out.

33.

34.

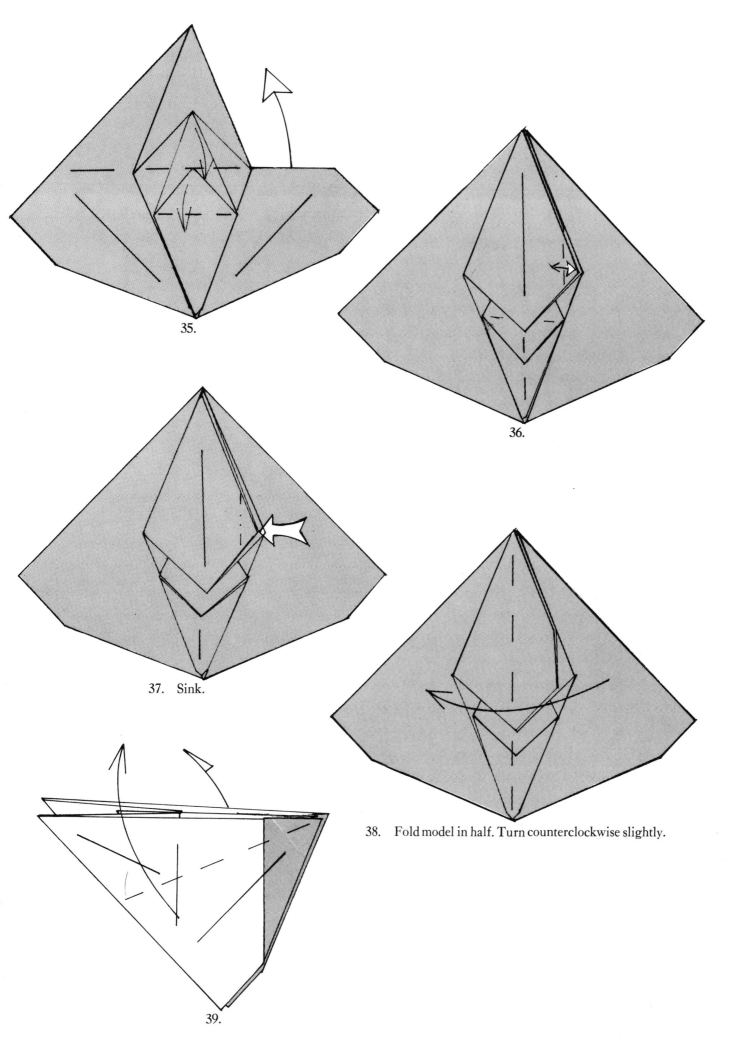

35.

36.

37. Sink.

38. Fold model in half. Turn counterclockwise slightly.

39.

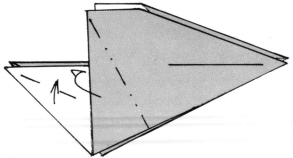

40. Reverse-fold; repeat behind.

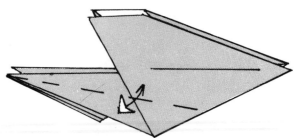

41. Fold and unfold; repeat behind.

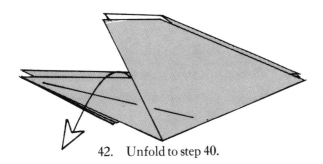

42. Unfold to step 40.

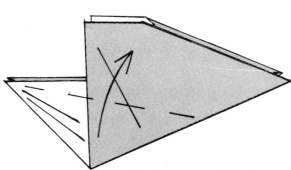

43. Fold along guidelines; repeat behind.

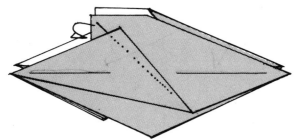

44. Mountain-fold; repeat behind.

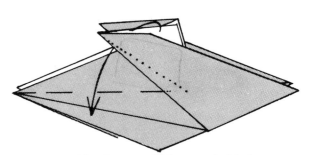

45. Reverse-fold; repeat behind.

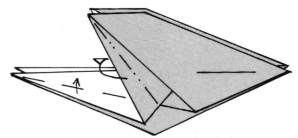

46. Reverse-fold; repeat behind.

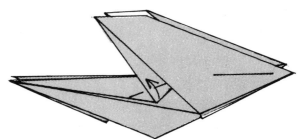

47. Valley-fold; repeat behind.

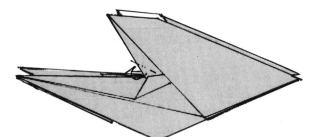

48. Mountain-fold; repeat behind.

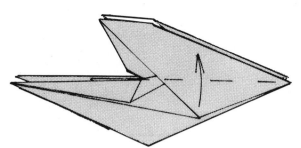

49. Valley-fold; repeat behind.

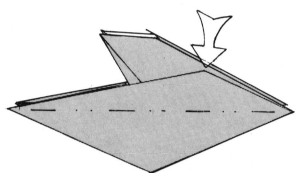

50. Sink; repeat behind.

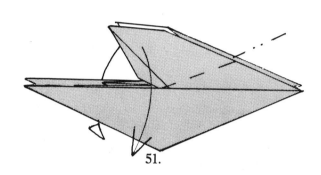

51.

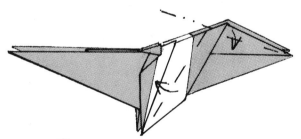

52. Valley-folds; repeat behind.

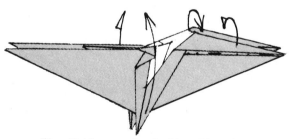

53. Fold upper flap inside, while folding wings up.

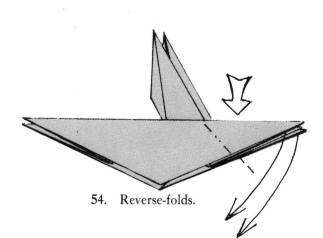

54. Reverse-folds.

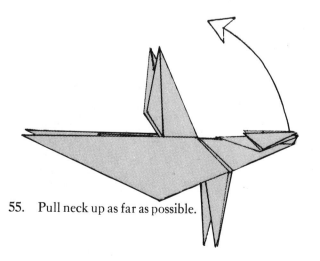

55. Pull neck up as far as possible.

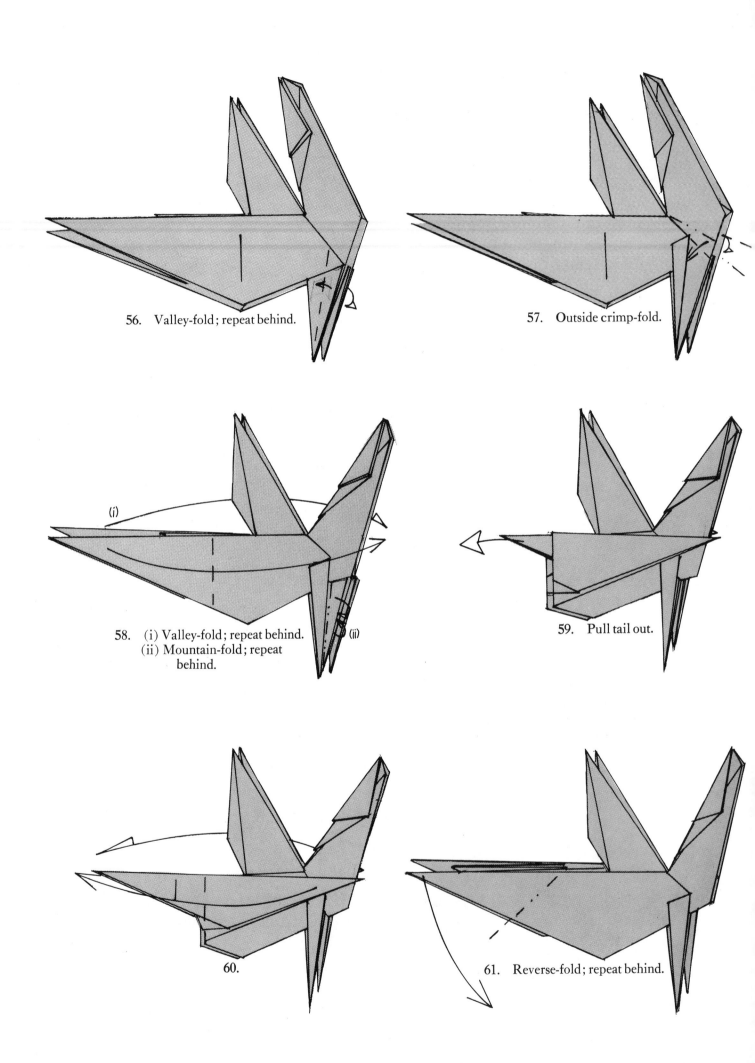

56.   Valley-fold; repeat behind.

57.   Outside crimp-fold.

58.   (i) Valley-fold; repeat behind.
       (ii) Mountain-fold; repeat
            behind.

59.   Pull tail out.

60.

61.   Reverse-fold; repeat behind.

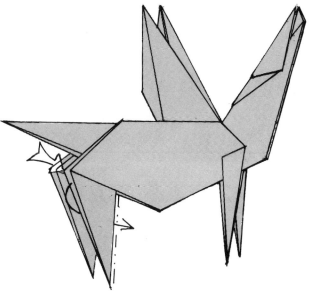

62.　Reverse-fold inside of leg; repeat behind.

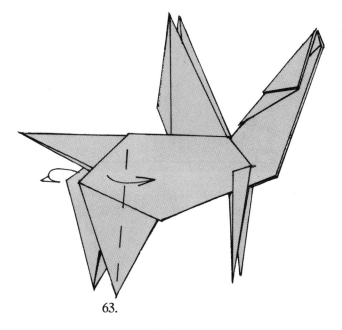

63.

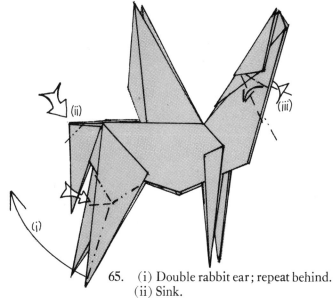

64.　(i) Outside crimp-fold.
　　(ii) Fold inside; repeat behind.

65.　(i) Double rabbit ear; repeat behind.
　　(ii) Sink.
　　(iii) Outside crimp-fold.

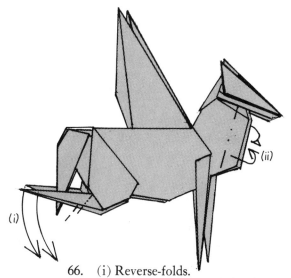

66.　(i) Reverse-folds.
　　(ii) Fold inside; repeat behind.

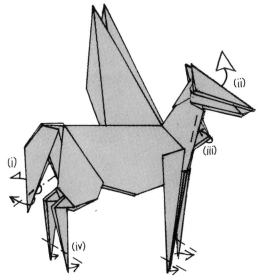

67.　(i) Outside reverse-fold tail.
　　(ii) Pull up two layers from behind head.
　　(iii) Tuck inside.
　　(iv) Reverse-fold to form feet.

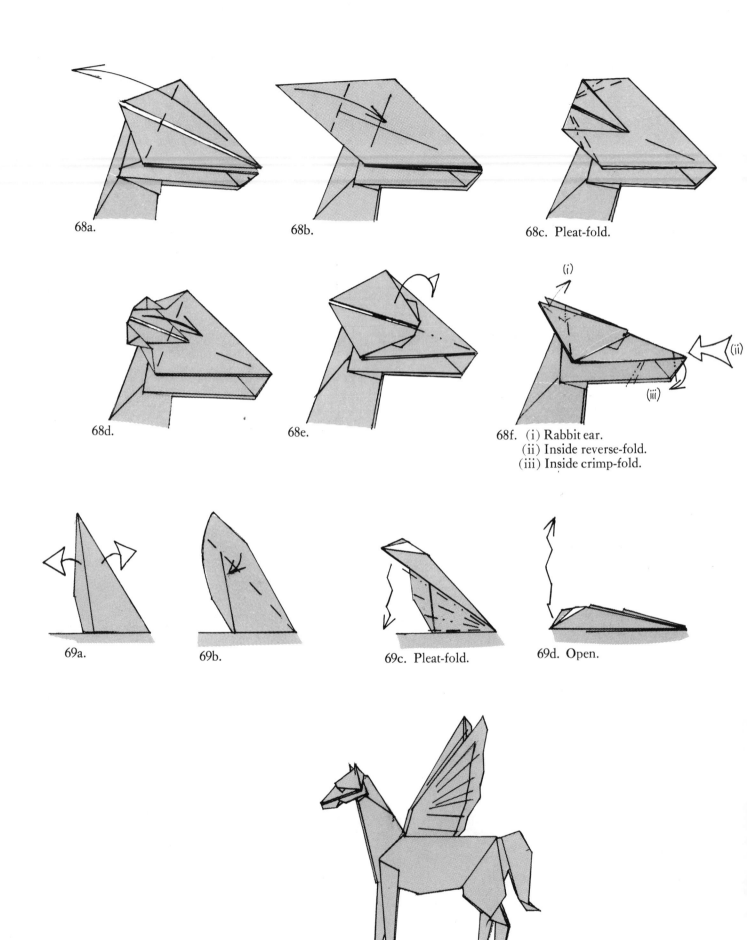

68a.

68b.

68c. Pleat-fold.

68d.

68e.

68f. (i) Rabbit ear.
(ii) Inside reverse-fold.
(iii) Inside crimp-fold.

(i)

(ii)

(iii)

69a.

69b.

69c. Pleat-fold.

69d. Open.

70. PEGASUS

MOTH

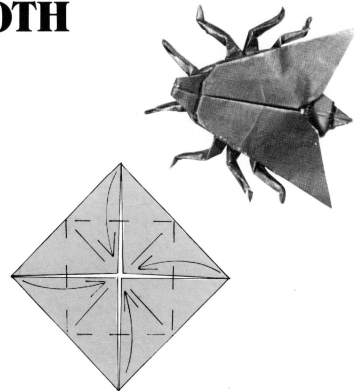

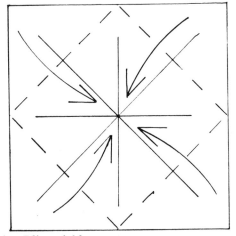

1. Blintz-fold.

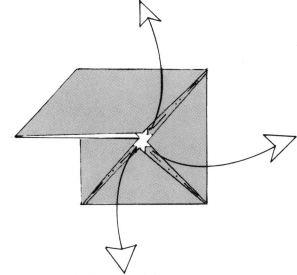

2. Blintz-fold again.

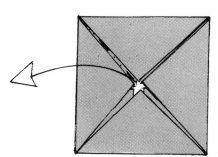

3. Pull out one corner.

4. Pull out remaining corners.

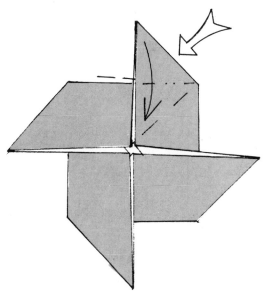

5. Squash-fold.

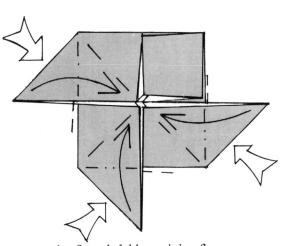

6. Squash-fold remaining flaps.

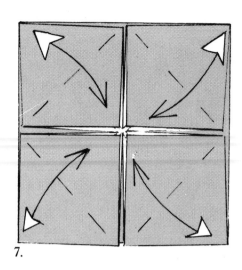

7.

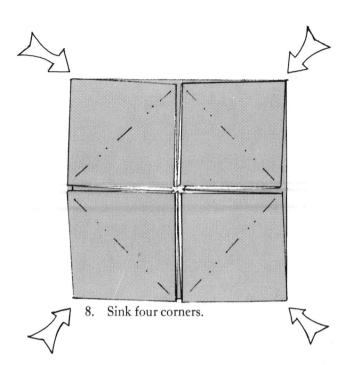

8. Sink four corners.

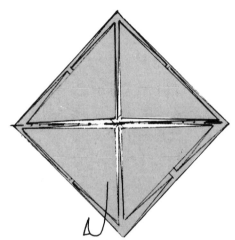

9. Mountain-fold model in half.

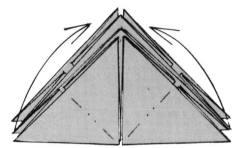

10. Reverse-fold middle flaps.

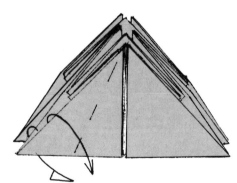

11. Outside reverse-fold.

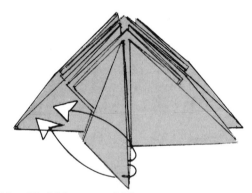

12. Unfold reverse-fold.

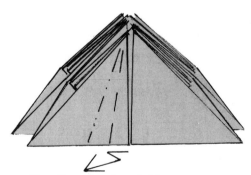

13. Outside crimp-fold.

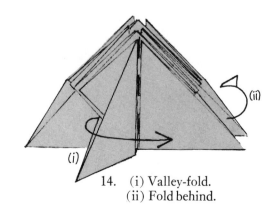

14. (i) Valley-fold.
(ii) Fold behind.

15. Repeat steps 11–13 on left side.

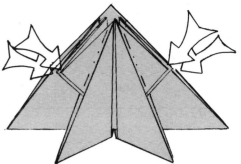

16. Reverse-folds.

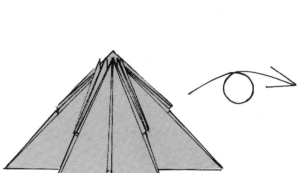

17.

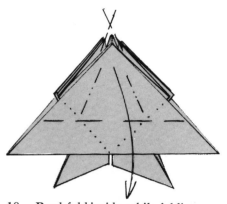

18. Petal-fold inside, while folding outer flap down.

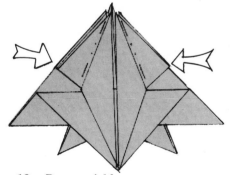

19. Reverse-folds.

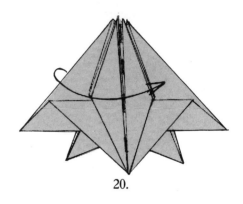

20.

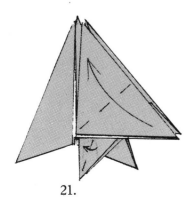

21.

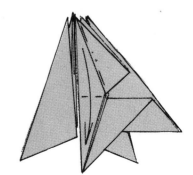

22. Petal-fold.

Moth 101

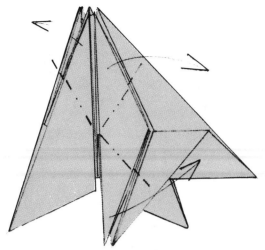

23. Reverse-fold 3 legs as shown.

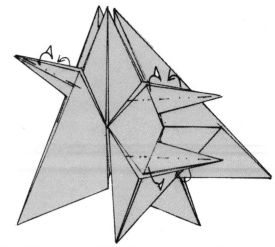

24. Mountain-fold inside; repeat behind.

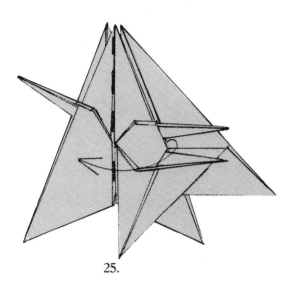

25.

26. Repeat steps 20–25 on right side.

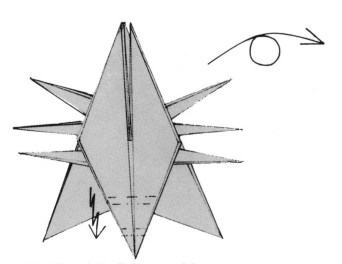

27. Pleat-fold tail. Turn model over.

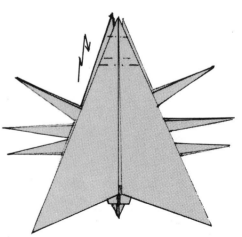

28. Pleat-fold to form head.

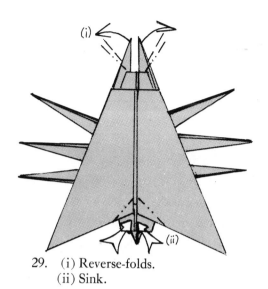

29. (i) Reverse-folds.
    (ii) Sink.

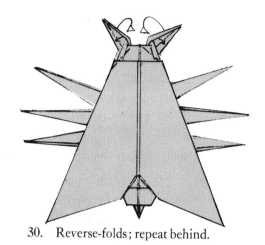

30. Reverse-folds; repeat behind.

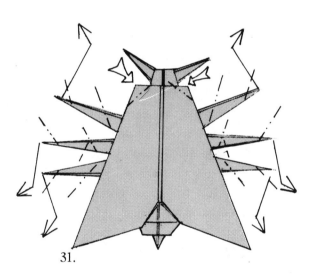

31.

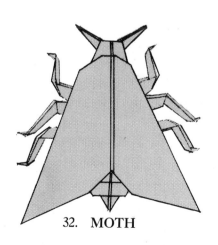

32. **MOTH**

STINK BUG

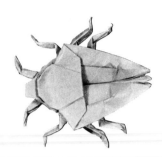

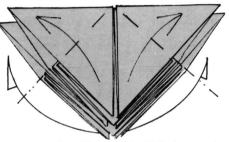

1. Begin with step 11 of Moth turned clockwise. Valley-fold; repeat behind.

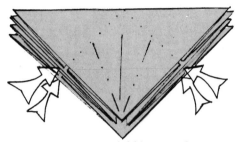

2. Reverse-fold lower 4 flaps.

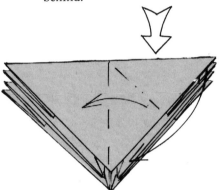

3. Squash-fold.

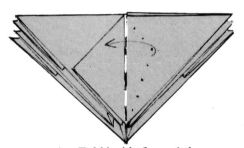

4. Fold inside flap to left.

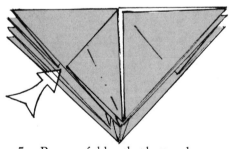

5. Reverse-fold so that bottom layer covers inside flap in step 4.

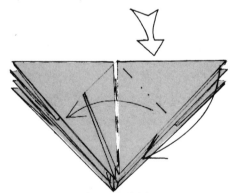

6. Squash-fold.

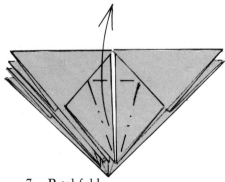

7. Petal-fold.

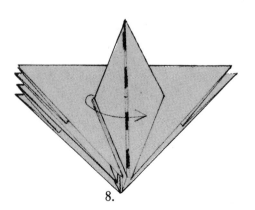

8.

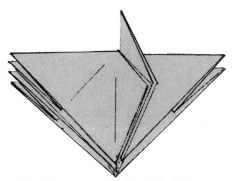

9. Repeat steps 3–8 on left side.

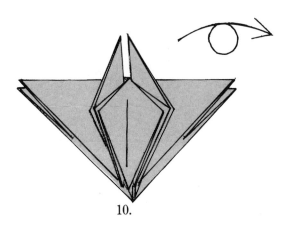

10.

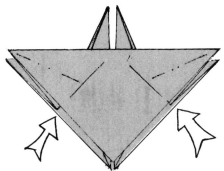

11. Reverse-folds.

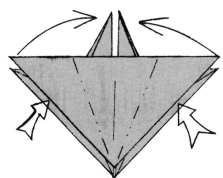

12. Reverse-folds.

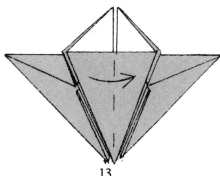

13.

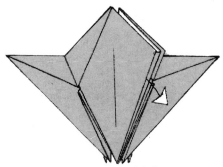

14. Pull out inside layer.

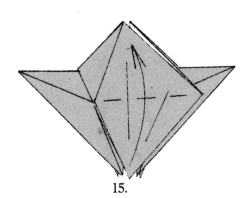

15.

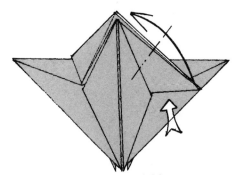

16. Reverse-fold.

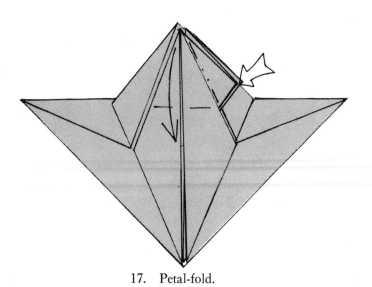

17. Petal-fold.

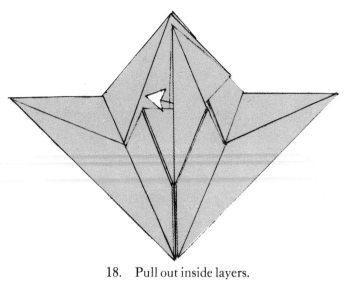

18. Pull out inside layers.

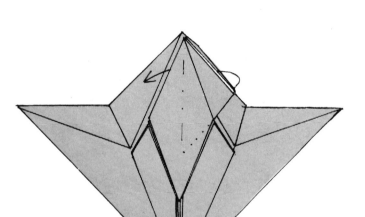
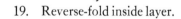

19. Reverse-fold inside layer.

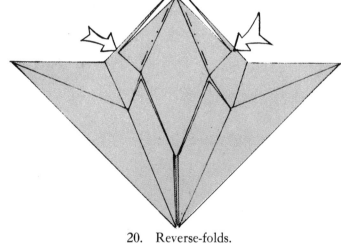

20. Reverse-folds.

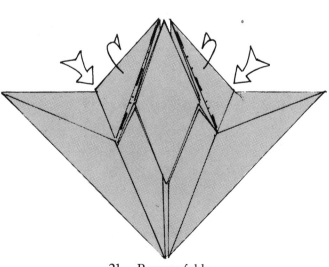

21. Reverse-folds.

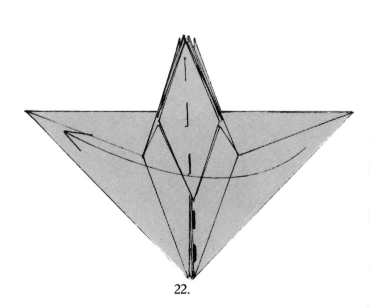

22.

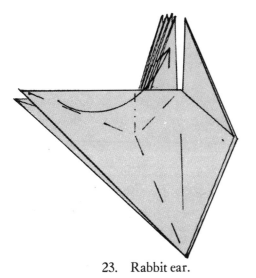

23. Rabbit ear.

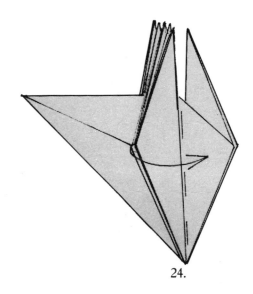

24.

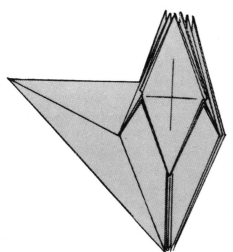

25. Repeat steps 22–24 on left side.

26.

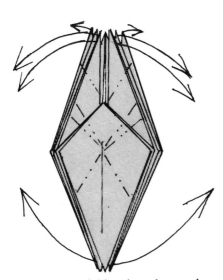

27. Reverse-fold to form legs and antennae.

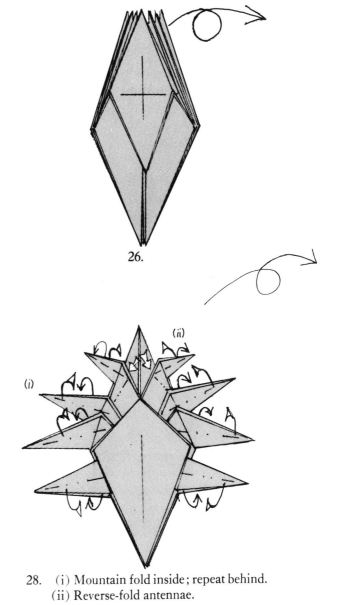

28. (i) Mountain fold inside; repeat behind.
(ii) Reverse-fold antennae.

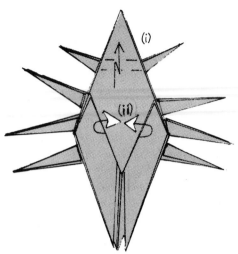

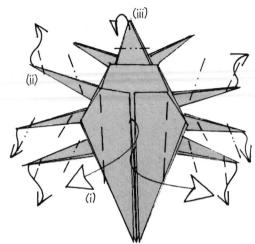

29. (i) Pleat-fold.
    (ii) Pull wings out and fold on top.

30. (i) Fold wings out.
    (ii) Reverse-fold each leg twice.
    (iii) Mountain-fold.

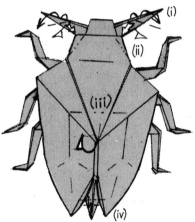

31. (i) Outside reverse-fold.
    (ii) Reverse-fold.
    (iii) Tuck under.
    (iv) Pleat-fold tail.

32. **STINK BUG**

BEETLE

1. Begin with step 11 of Stink bug. Fold model in half.

2.

3. Reverse-fold.

4. Unfold.

5. Repeat steps 1–4 on right side.

6. Reverse-folds.

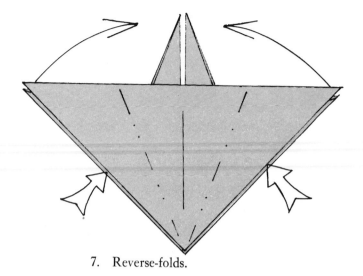

7. Reverse-folds.

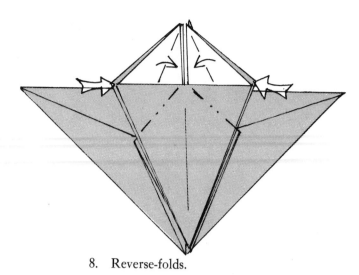

8. Reverse-folds.

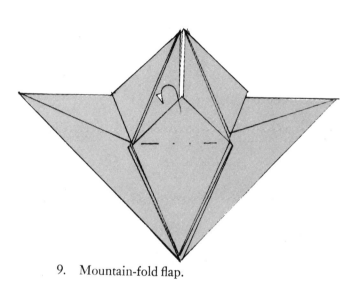

9. Mountain-fold flap.

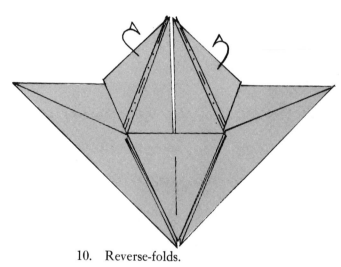

10. Reverse-folds.

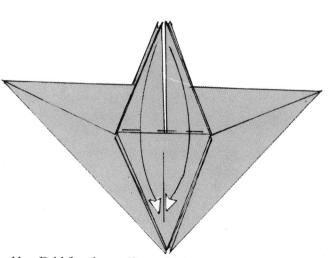

11. Fold flap down. (Several folds will open.)

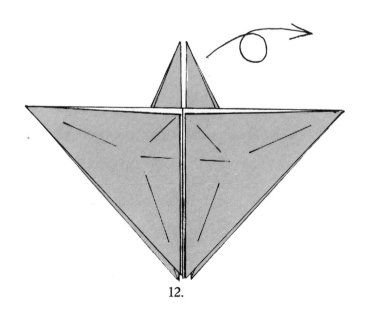

12.

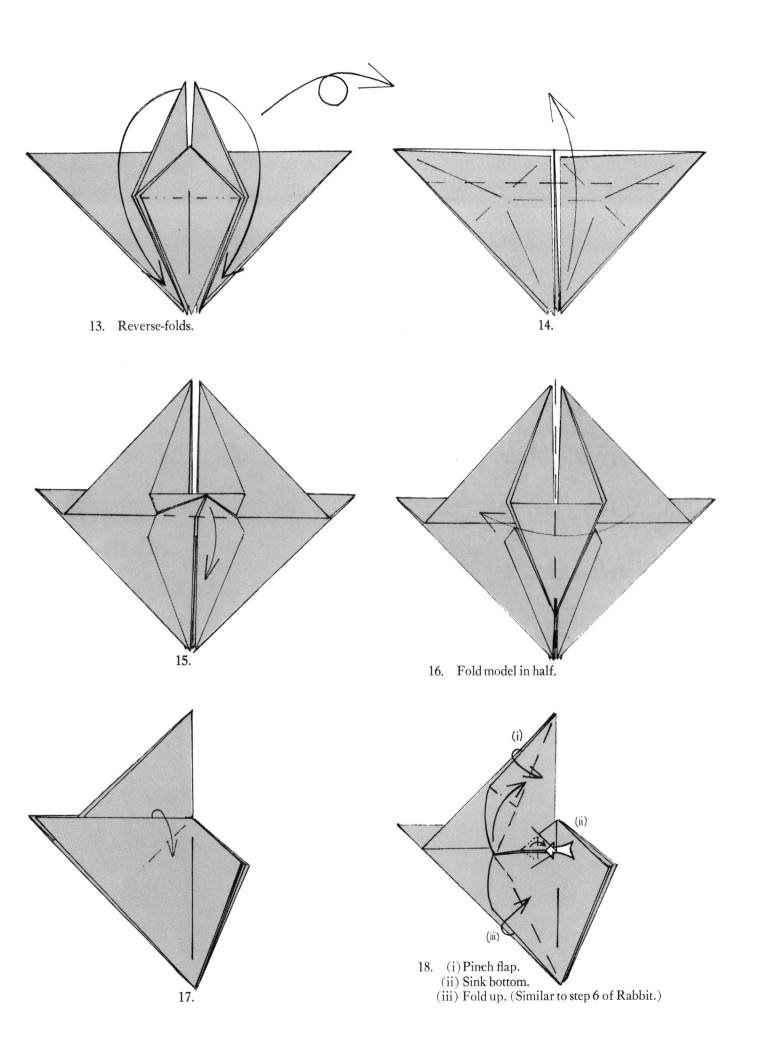

13.   Reverse-folds.

14.

15.

16.   Fold model in half.

17.

18.   (i) Pinch flap.
      (ii) Sink bottom.
      (iii) Fold up. (Similar to step 6 of Rabbit.)

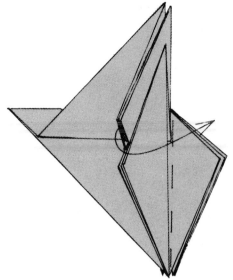

19. Repeat steps 16–19 on left side.

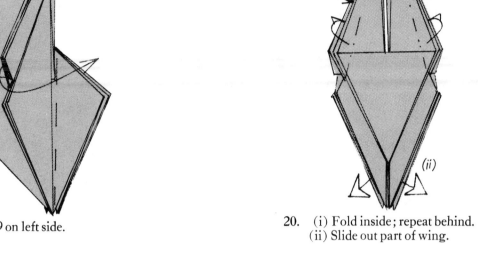

20. (i) Fold inside; repeat behind.
    (ii) Slide out part of wing.

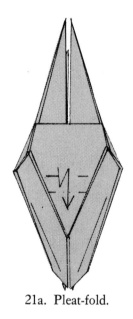

21a. Pleat-fold.

21b. Squash-folds.

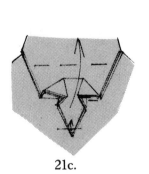

21c.

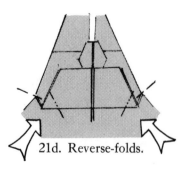

21d. Reverse-folds.

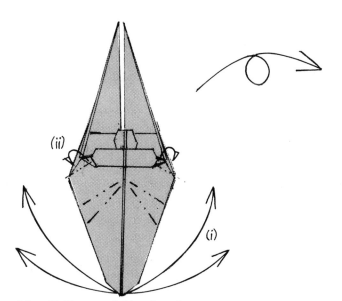

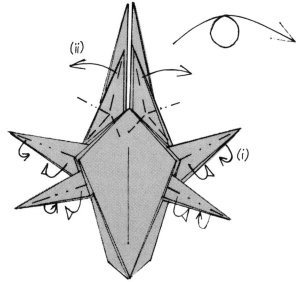

22. (i) Reverse-fold to form legs.
    (ii) Tuck inside. Turn model over.

23. (i) Mountain-fold inside; repeat behind
        on remaining back legs.
    (ii) Rabbit ear. Turn model over.

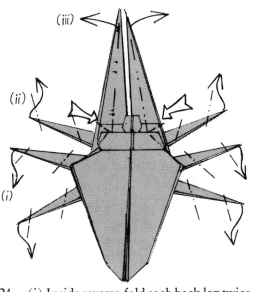

24. (i) Inside reverse-fold each back leg twice.
    (ii) Outside reverse-fold each front leg twice.
    (iii) Double rabbit ear antennae.

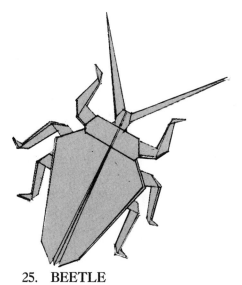

25. **BEETLE**

GRASSHOPPER

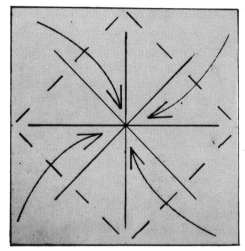

1. . Blintz-fold.

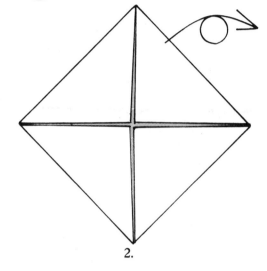

2.

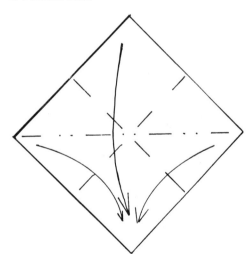

3.   Preliminary-fold.

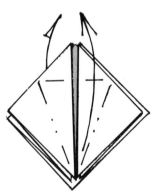

4.   Petal-fold front and back.

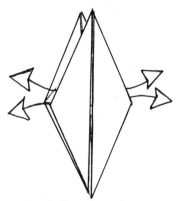

5.   Pull out inner layers.

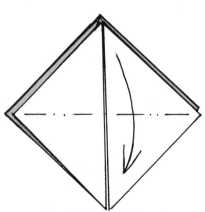

6.   Valley-fold front layer.

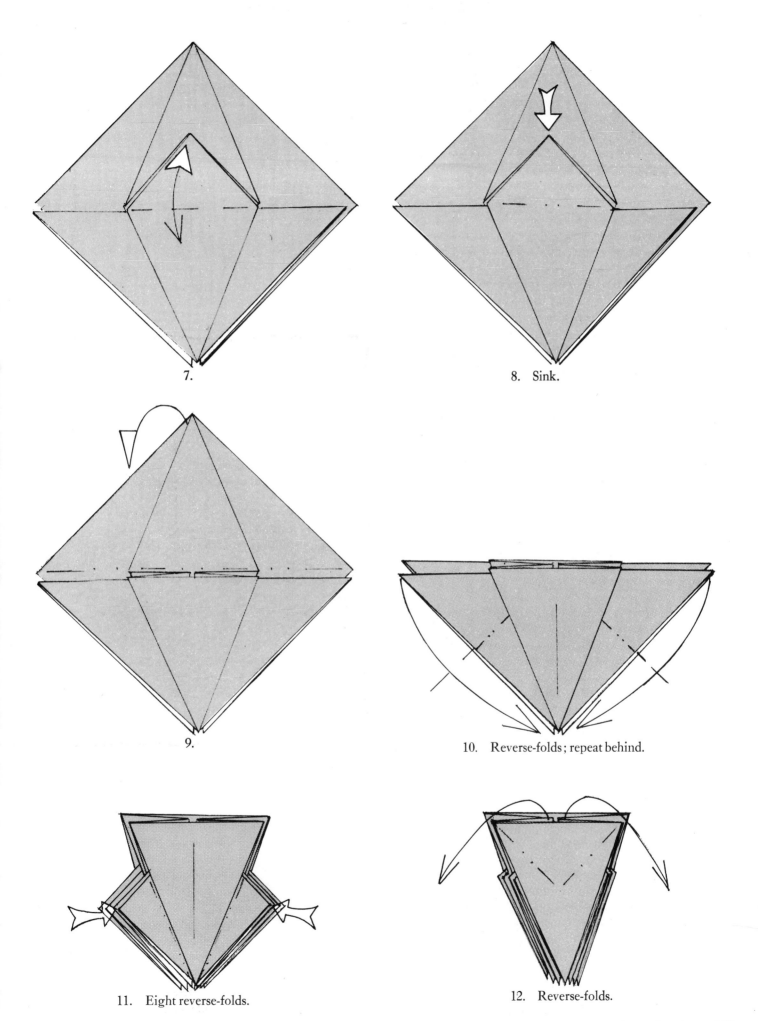

7.

8. Sink.

9.

10. Reverse-folds; repeat behind.

11. Eight reverse-folds.

12. Reverse-folds.

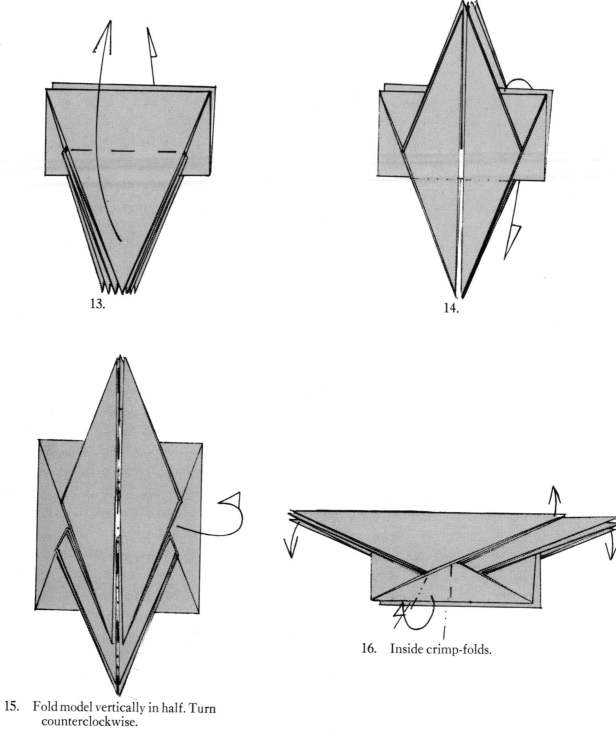

13.

14.

15. Fold model vertically in half. Turn counterclockwise.

16. Inside crimp-folds.

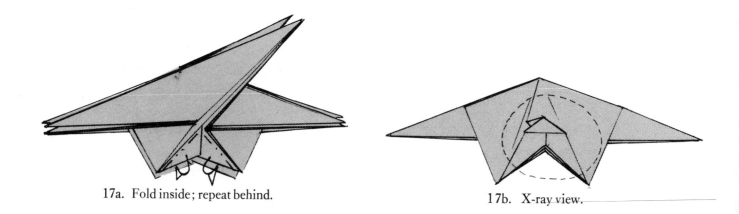

17a. Fold inside; repeat behind.

17b. X-ray view.

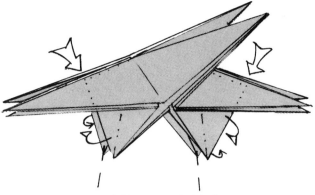

18. Reverse-folds; repeat behind.

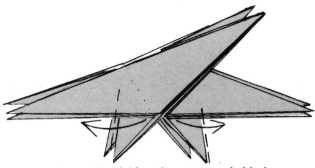

19. Valley-fold top layer; repeat behind.

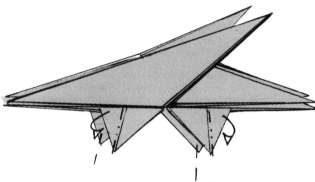

20. Mountain-fold; repeat behind.

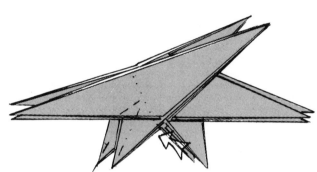

21. Reverse-fold lowest layer of top flaps; repeat behind.

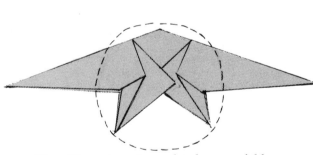

21a. X-ray view of completed reverse-folds.

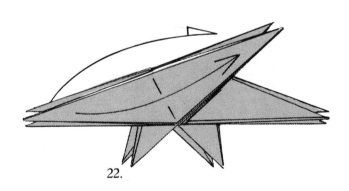

22.

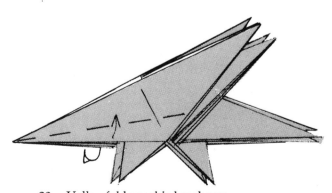

23. Valley-fold one third as shown.

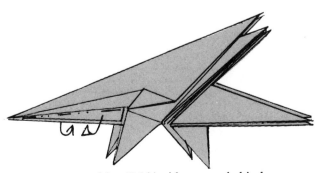

24. Fold inside; repeat behind.

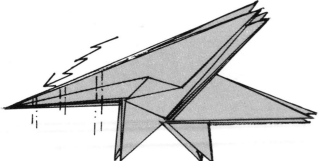

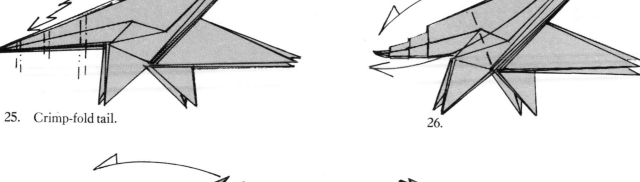

25. Crimp-fold tail.

26.

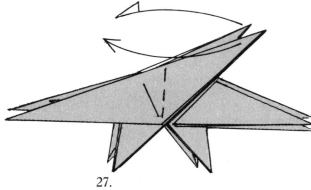

27.

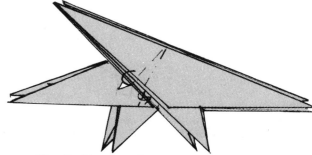

28. Inside crimp-fold; repeat behind.

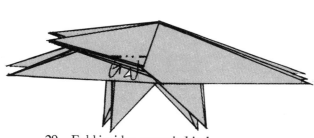

29. Fold inside; repeat behind.

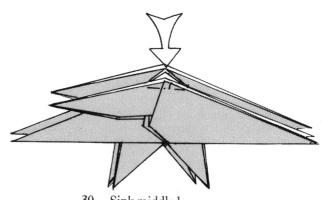

30. Sink middle layer.

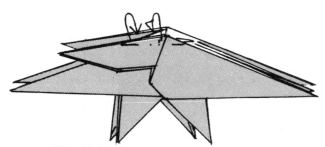

31. Fold inside; repeat behind.

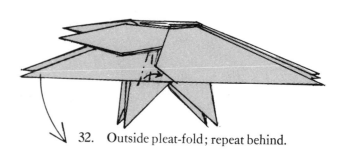

32. Outside pleat-fold; repeat behind.

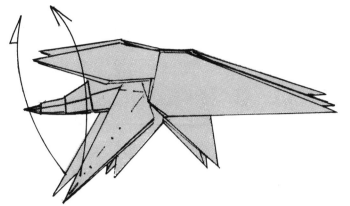

33. Petal-fold; repeat behind.

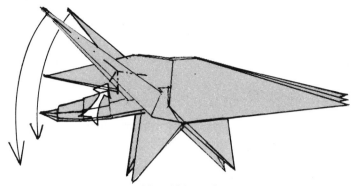

34. Double rabbit ear legs.

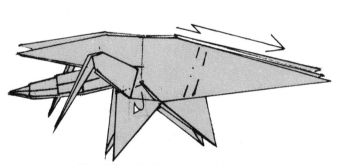

35. Pleat-fold; repeat behind.

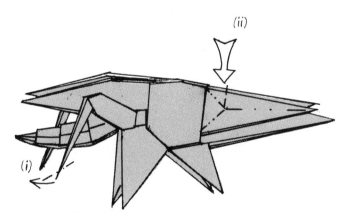

(ii)

(i)

36. (i) Reverse-fold; repeat behind.
    (ii) Double rabbit ear; repeat behind.

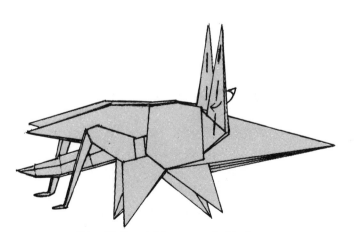

37. Valley-folds; repeat behind.

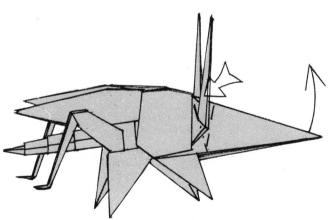

38. Inside crimp-fold head.

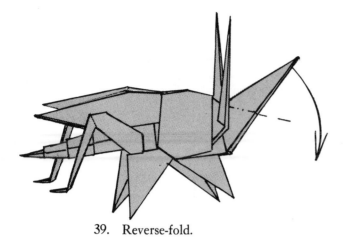

39. Reverse-fold.

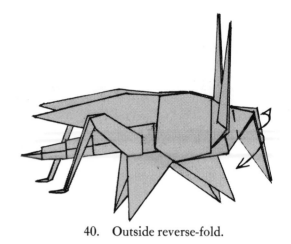

40. Outside reverse-fold.

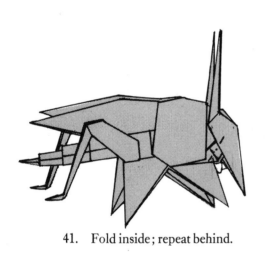

41. Fold inside; repeat behind.

42. (i) Double rabbit ear legs; repeat behind.
(ii) Crimp-fold mouth.

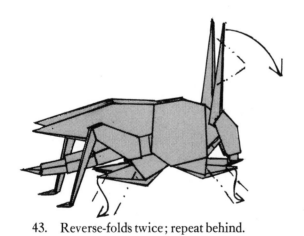

43. Reverse-folds twice; repeat behind.

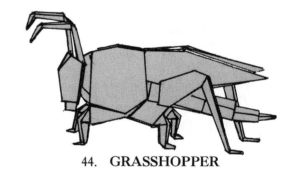

44. **GRASSHOPPER**